Name ______________________ Date ______________

W9-DJP-118

Uses of Numbers

Answer each question about animals in space.

1. In November 1957, a dog named Laika became the first animal ever launched into outer space. Which number in these space facts is ordinal? How is it used?

   first; to show position

2. The satellite that carried Laika into space was called *Sputnik 2*. This spacecraft weighed about 1,120 pounds. Which number in these space facts is used to measure?

   1,120

3. Between 1958 and 1960, the United States launched 4 monkeys into space. Their names were Gordo, Able, Baker, and Sam. Which number is used to count?

   4

4. *Sputnik 5* was launched in 1960. On board were 2 dogs named Belka and Strelka, 40 mice, and 2 rats. What numbers in these facts are NOT used to count? How are those numbers used?

   1960 and 5 (in Sputnik); to label

5. A chimpanzee named Ham flew a United States space flight test in 1961. During his trip, Ham experienced 7 minutes of weightlessness. How is the number 7 used in these facts?

   to measure time

Use with text pages 4–5.

Name ______________________ Date ____________

Problem Solving 1.2

Place Value: Ones, Tens, Hundreds

Use Data Use the table to solve.

There have been a total of 6 missions in which astronauts landed on the moon. The length of each of those missions is shown in the table below.

Time in Outer Space	
Mission	**Hours**
Apollo 11	195 hours
Apollo 12	245 hours
Apollo 14	216 hours
Apollo 15	295 hours
Apollo 16	266 hours
Apollo 17	302 hours

1. In 1969, the *Apollo 11* astronauts became the first people to land on the moon. How would you write the number of hours for their mission in expanded form? In word form?

   100 + 90 + 5; one hundred ninety-five

2. Which mission's length has the same digit in the tens place and the ones place?

   Apollo 16

3. **Reasoning** The length of my Apollo mission is an odd 3-digit number. The digit in the tens place is twice the hundreds digit. On which Apollo mission did I serve?

   Apollo 12

4. **You Decide** Ken says that the *Apollo 14* mission was in outer space for about 200 hours. Bill says it was in outer space for about 300 hours. Who do you think is correct? Explain your choice.

   Ken is correct. *Explanations may vary.*

Use with text pages 6–7.

Name ______________________ Date ____________

How Big Is One Thousand?

The Space Museum store sells glow-in-the-dark star stickers in the packages shown below. For Problems 1–5, tell if each person bought *more than 1,000, less than 1,000,* or *exactly 1,000* star stickers.

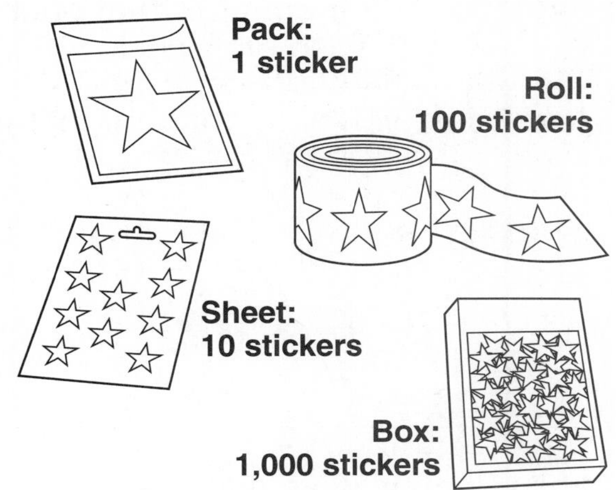

1. Tim bought 5 rolls of star stickers.

   less than 1,000

2. Carol bought 9 boxes of star stickers.

   more than 1,000

3. Anita bought 10 rolls of star stickers.

   exactly 1,000

4. Jamal bought 10 sheets of star stickers.

   less than 1,000

5. **What If?** Kelly wants to put 1,000 star stickers on her bedroom ceiling. If Kelly got 5 rolls of star stickers for her birthday, how many more stickers would she need to buy? How many more rolls of stickers would she need to buy? How many more sheets of stickers?

   500 more stickers;
   5 more rolls;
   50 more sheets

Show your work.

Use

Name ________________________ Date ____________

Problem Solving 1.4

Place Value Through Thousands

Use Data Use the table to solve.

Scientists describe the size of a planet or a moon by its diameter, or the distance across its middle. The table below shows the diameters of the largest moons in our solar system and the planet that each moon orbits.

Moon Sizes		
Moon	**Planet**	**Diameter**
Callisto	Jupiter	2,984 miles
Europa	Jupiter	1,944 miles
Ganymede	Jupiter	3,272 miles
Io	Jupiter	2,262 miles
Moon	Earth	2,160 miles
Titan	Saturn	3,198 miles
Triton	Neptune	1,680 miles

1. Find the diameter of Earth's moon. How would you write that number in expanded form? In word form?

   2,000 + 100 + 60; two thousand, one hundred sixty

2. Which moons have diameters less than two thousand miles long?

   Europa and Triton

3. Which moons' diameters have a 2 in the hundreds place?

   Ganymede and Io

4. **Reasoning** I am one of Jupiter's moons. My diameter does not have a 2 in the thousands place. The digit in the tens place is the same as the ones digit. Which moon am I?

   Europa

5. **Reasoning** Our diameters have the same digit in the thousands place. Our diameters also have the same digit in the tens place. Which moons are we?

   Io and Moon

6. **What's Wrong?** Carla says that the diameter of Triton is one thousand sixty-eight miles long. Why is she wrong?

   Answers may vary.

7. **What If?** If the diameter of a moon in whole miles has exactly 4 digits, what is the greatest diameter that moon could have?

   9,999 miles

Name ______________________ Date __________

Problem Solving 1.5

Problem-Solving Strategy: Find a Number Pattern

Problem We measure one year by the time it takes Earth to orbit the sun. To make our calendars match Earth's exact orbit time, we have leap years. Leap years add one extra day to the year. In the 21st century, the first four leap years are 2000, 2004, 2008, and 2012. Following this pattern, what will be the fifth leap year in the 21st century?

UNDERSTAND

1. Which facts in the problem can you use to answer that question?
The first four leap years are 2000, 2004, 2008, and 2012.

PLAN

2. Do the given leap year numbers increase or decrease? What does this tell you about the fifth leap year number?
increase; it will be greater than the fourth leap year number.

SOLVE

3. Continue the pattern to find the fifth leap year. 2012 + 4 = 2016; the fifth leap year will be 2016.

LOOK BACK

4. What other strategies could you have used to solve the problem?
Answers may vary.

Name ______________________ Date ____________

Problem Solving 1.6

Place Value Through Ten Thousands

Use Data Use the table to solve.

How Fast the Planets Orbit, or Travel Around, the Sun	
Planet	**Average Speed**
Mercury	107,082 mph
Venus	78,338 mph
Earth	66,616 mph
Mars	53,977 mph
Jupiter	29,237 mph
Saturn	21,676 mph
Uranus	15,234 mph
Neptune	12,147 mph
Pluto	10,558 mph

1. Look at how many miles per hour Venus travels around the sun. Write that number in expanded form.

   70,000 + 8,000 + 300 + 30 + 8

2. Which planets travel at average speeds of less than 20,000 miles per hour?

   Uranus, Neptune, and Pluto

3. Which planet's average speed has the same digit in the ten thousands place, the thousands place, and the hundreds place?

   Earth

4. Which planet orbits the sun at an average speed of fifty-three thousand, nine hundred seventy-seven miles per hour?

   Mars

5. **Estimate** Which planet travels around the sun about twice as fast as Pluto travels around the sun?

   Saturn

Use with text pages 18–19.

Name ______________________ Date ____________

Problem Solving 1.7

Place Value Through Hundred Thousands

Use Data Use the table to solve.

Gravity is what causes objects to have weight. Gravity is different on each planet. So the weights of objects are also different. The table below shows how much the International Space Station would weigh on each planet in our solar system.

How Much Does the International Space Station Weigh on Different Planets?	
Planet	**Weight**
Mercury	155,299 pounds
Venus	372,637 pounds
Earth	410,846 pounds
Mars	154,889 pounds
Jupiter	971,240 pounds
Saturn	376,335 pounds
Uranus	365,242 pounds
Neptune	462,202 pounds
Pluto	27,526 pounds

1. Write the space station's weight on Earth in expanded form and in word form.

   400,000 + 10,000 + 800 + 40 + 6; 410,846 four hundred ten thousand, eight hundred forty-six

2. On which planets would the space station weigh less than two hundred thousand pounds?

   Mercury, Mars, and Pluto

3. On which planets does the weight of the space station have the same digit in the tens place and the hundred thousands place?

   Venus, Earth, and Saturn

4. On which planets would the space station weigh between one hundred thousand and two hundred thousand pounds?

   Mercury and Mars

5. Find the planet on which the spa station would weigh the most. would you write that number pounds in word form?

   nine hundred one thousan hundred fo

Use w

Name ______________________ Date ______________

Problem Solving 2.1

Compare Numbers

Use Data Use the table to solve.

Daily Television Viewing Times	
Country	**Number of Minutes**
Belgium	177
Canada	194
France	187
Germany	188
Greece	219
Ireland	194
Italy	216
Spain	211
United Kingdom	216
United States	238

1. In which country is the daily viewing time greater, France or Germany?

   Germany

2. In which country is the daily viewing time less, Italy or Greece?

   Italy

3. There are 180 minutes in 3 hours. Which country has a daily viewing time of less than 3 hours?

   Belgium

4. **Reasoning** Our countries have a daily viewing time of more than 200 minutes. We have the same daily viewing times. What countries are we?

   Italy and the United Kingdom

5. **Reasoning** Our countries have a daily viewing time of less than 200 minutes. We have the same daily viewing times. What countries are we?

   Canada and Ireland

Use with text pages 28–29.

Name ______________________ Date ____________

Problem Solving 2.2

Order Numbers

Use Data Use the table below for Problems 1–3.

Shakespeare Festival Ticket Sales	
Play	**Number of Tickets**
Hamlet	496
Much Ado About Nothing	512
Romeo and Juliet	469
The Taming of the Shrew	460

1. Order the number of tickets sold for each play from least to greatest.

   460; 469; 496; 512

2. Which play had the greatest number of tickets sold? Which had the least?

   Much Ado About Nothing; The Taming of the Shrew

3. **What If?** Suppose ten more tickets were sold for *The Taming of the Shrew.* Would this affect your answer for Problem 2? Explain your thinking.

   Yes; Explanations may vary.

Use Data Use the table below for Problems 4–5.

Shakespeare's Longest Plays	
Play	**Number of Lin**
Coriolanus	3,820
Cymbeline	3,81[illegible]
Hamlet	3[illegible]
Othello	[illegible]
Richard III	[illegible]

4. Order the number of lines from greatest to least for the plays *Coriolanus, Cymbeline,* and *Richard III.*

   3,886; 3,820; 3,813

5. **You Decide** Emma says that she does not have to compare the digits in the ones place to solve Problem 2. Do you agree? Explain your answer.

   Yes; Explanations may vary.

Name ______________________ Date ____________

Problem Solving 2.3

Round Two-Digit and Three-Digit Numbers

Use Data Use the table to solve.

Countries That Make the Most Movies	
Country	**Movies Made in a Recent Year**
India	764
United States	628
Japan	270
Philippines	220
France	181
Hong Kong	146
Italy	108
Spain	97
United Kingdom	92
China	85

1. How many movies were made in the United States? What is that number rounded to the nearest ten? To the nearest hundred?

   628 movies; about 630; about 600

2. Which countries' number of movies are about 200 when rounded to the nearest hundred?

   the Philippines and France

3. Which countries' number of movies seem to be already rounded to the nearest ten? How do you know?

   Japan and the Philippines

4. **Reasoning** When my number of movies is rounded to the nearest ten, it is 50 more than my number of movies rounded to the nearest hundred. What country am I?

   Hong Kong

5. **Write About It** When rounded to the nearest ten, a number is 100. Does this mean that the original number must be a three-digit number? Use one of the numbers in the table to explain your answer.

   No; *Explanations may vary.*

Use with text pages 32–34.

Name ____________________ Date __________

Problem Solving 2.4

Round Four-Digit Numbers

Use Data Use the table to solve.

Longest-Running Broadway Shows*	
Show	**Number of Performances**
Cats	7,485
Les Misérables	6,276
A Chorus Line	6,137
The Phantom of the Opera	5,979
Oh! Calcutta!	5,959
Miss Saigon	4,092
42nd Street	3,486
Grease	3,388
Fiddler on the Roof	3,242
Life with Father	3,224

* as of 2002

1. What is the longest-running Broadway show? Rounded to the nearest hundred, how many times was the show performed?

   Cats; about 7,500 times

2. Rounded to the nearest thousand, which shows were performed about 6,000 times?

   Les Miserables, A Chorus Line, Oh! Calcutta!, and The Phantom of the Opera

3. Which two shows have the same number of performances when rounded to the nearest thousand **and** when rounded to the nearest hundred?

   Oh! Calcutta! and The Phantom of the Opera

4. **Reasoning** When rounded to the nearest ten, my number of performances ends in the digits 90. I am not *42nd Street, Cats or Miss Saigon.* What show am I?

   Grease

5. **What's the Question?** is about 4,100 times. W about the data in the have been asked?

   Questio

Use wi

Name ______________________ Date ____________

Problem Solving 2.5

Problem-Solving Application: Use a Bar Graph

The graph on the right shows the number of radio stations in the United States that follow four popular formats. Which format has the most stations? How many radio stations in the United States follow that format?

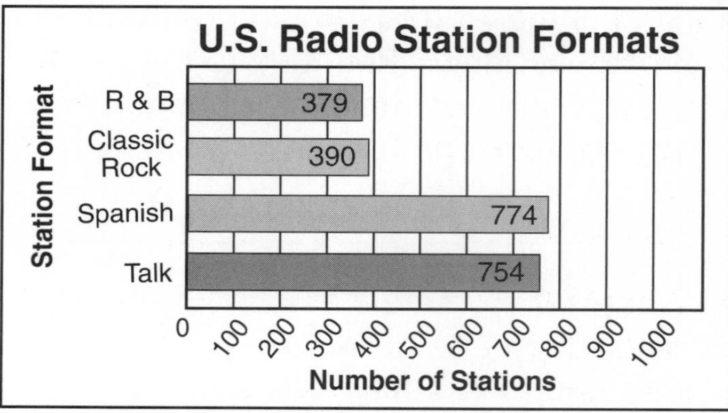

UNDERSTAND

1. What facts do you need to answer the questions?

I need the number of stations for each of the four formats.

PLAN

2. How can you use the bar graph to solve the problem?

Answers may vary.

SOLVE

3. Write the solution to the problem in complete sentences.

The Spanish radio format has the most stations. There are 774 radio stations in the United States that follow the Spanish format.

ACK

4. Could you have solved the problem without using the bar graph? Explain.

No; Answers may vary.

Name ______________________ Date __________

Value of Money

Answer each question.

1. Antoine needs change for a gumball machine. He has 2 one-dollar bills. How many pennies can he get if he gets only pennies? How many dimes can he get if he gets only dimes?

   200 pennies; 20 dimes

2. What is the greatest amount of money you can have that is less than one dollar? Write that amount, using a dollar sign and a decimal point.

   $0.99

3. **What's Wrong?** At her yard sale, Linda wanted to charge five dollars and four cents for a board game. She wrote $5.40 on the game's price tag. What is wrong with the price tag? *Answers may vary. Sample:* The amount on the price tag is incorrect, because $5.40 is five dollars and forty cents. She should have written $5.04 on the price tag.

4. **Reasoning** Chen had the money shown below in her purse. She spent half of the dimes on a magazine. What is the value of the money left in her purse?

   $2.39

Name ______________________ Date ____________

Problem Solving 3.2

Count Coins and Bills

Use Data Use the marble sale sign for Problems 1–4.

MARBLE SALE	
Type of Marble	Price
Shooter	$ 1.70
Agate	$ 2.75
Steely	$ 1.55
Cat's Eye	$ 0.89
Butterfly	$ 1.05

1. Sara paid for a marble with a one-dollar bill, 2 quarters, 1 dime, 1 nickel, and 5 pennies. What type of marble did she buy?

   shooter

2. Kenji bought two marbles. He paid for the marbles with 3 one-dollar bills and 8 dimes. What marbles did he buy?

   agate and butterfly

3. **You Decide** What coins would you use to exactly pay for a cat's eye marble?

   Answers may vary.

4. **Reasoning** Ted used only quarters to pay the exact price of one marble. Which marble did Ted buy?

   agate

5. **Reasoning** Tameeka has 4 coins. Only two of the coins are the same. What is the greatest amount of money Tameeka can have? What is the least amount?

   $1.35; $0.17

Name ______________________ Date ____________

Problem Solving 3.3

Problem-Solving Application: Make Change

Problem Julio buys a slice of pizza for $1.68. He gives the cashier a five-dollar bill. How much change should Julio receive?

UNDERSTAND

1. What do you want to know?

How much change Julio should receive.

PLAN

2. How does the price of the pizza compare to the amount Julio paid?

The price of the pizza is less than the amount Julio paid.

SOLVE

3. What coins and bills did you use to count up?

Answers may vary.

4. How much change should Julio receive?

$3.32

LOOK BACK

5. How can you check that your answer is reasonable?

Samples: I can count back $3.32 fro[m] $5.00 to make sure I end at $1.68.

Name ______________________ Date ____________

Compare Money Amounts

Use Data Use the sign to solve.

1. Which ride at the state fair costs the most? Which ride costs the least?

   roller coaster; merry-go-round

2. Write the prices of the bumper cars, the water slide, and the tea cups in order from least to greatest.

   $1.50; $1.70; $1.75

3. Alvin wants to ride the pirate ship and the bumper cars. He has $5.00. Does he have enough money? How do you know?

   No. Sample: $4.50 + $1.50 = $6.00 and $6.00 > $5.00.

4. **What's Wrong?** Aleesha uses 3 one-dollar bills to pay for a ride on the Ferris wheel. She receives 3 dimes in change. What's wrong?

   She should receive 70¢ in change, not 30¢.

5. **Reasoning** Ryan used 5 coins to pay for a ride on the merry-go-round. He did not receive any change. What coins could Ryan have used?

   answers may vary; 3 quarters and 2 dimes

STATE FAIR RIDES

RIDE	PRICE
Roller Coaster	$4.75
Ferris Wheel	$2.30
Merry-Go-Round	$0.95
Bumper Cars	$1.50
Water Slide	$1.75
Pirate Ship	$4.50
Tea Cups	$1.70
Parachute	$4.70

Name ______________________ Date ____________

Problem Solving 3.5

Round Money

Use Data Use the table to solve.

In 1938, the United States government set the first law for minimum wage. Minimum wage is the least amount of money a worker can earn per hour. The table below shows the minimum wage during different years in the United States.

Minimum Wage Pay		
Year	**Hourly Pay**	**Daily Pay**
1950	$0.75	$6.00
1960	$1.00	$8.00
1970	$1.60	$12.80
1980	$3.10	$24.80
1990	$3.80	$30.40
2000	$5.15	$41.20

SOURCE: Minimum Wage: World Almanac and Book of Facts, 2002, p. 144.

1. In which year was the minimum wage about $3.00?

   1980

2. When did a minimum-wage worker earn about $40.00 a day?

   2000

3. In which year did a minimum-wage worker earn about $8.00 for working 2 hours?

   1990

4. **What's Wrong?** Calvin says that the minimum daily pay for 1970 rounded to the nearest ten dollars is $20.00. Explain why he is wrong.

   Sample: Rounded to the nearest ten dollars, $12.80 is $10.00, not $20.00.

5. Alexi says that a worker earned about $10.00 a day at minimum wage in 1960 and 1970. Why does she use the same amount for both years?

   Sample: She rounded both year's amounts to the nearest ten dollars.

Name ______________________ Date ______________

Problem Solving 4.1

Addition Properties

Use addition properties to answer each question about national parks.

1. There are 5 national parks in Louisiana. Mississippi has 7 national parks. Alabama has 5 national parks. Think about adding those three numbers. Which two numbers would you add first? Why?

   I would add 5 + 5 to make 10. Then I would add 10 + 7.

2. Alaska has 18 national parks. If you add zero to that number, you get the number of national parks in Virginia. How many national parks are in Virginia? How do you know?

   18 national parks; The sum of any number and zero is that number.

3. **Reasoning** California has more national parks than many other states. The sum of the two digits in its number of parks is 6. Both digits are even. If California has less than 30 national parks, how many does it have?

   24 national parks

4. **Write About It** Yellowstone National Park is so large that it stretches across Wyoming, Idaho, and Montana. To find how many National parks these three states have altogether, Shaneeka used 7 + 5 + 7. Tony used 5 + 7 + 7. Explain why they both got the same sum.

   Answers may vary.

Use with text pages 76–77.

Name ______________________ Date ____________

Problem Solving 4.2

Estimate Sums

Use Data Use the table to solve.

1. About how many pounds of peanuts and sunflower seeds combined are used each week?

   about 120 pounds

2. About how many pounds of bananas and barley combined are used each week?

   about 1,100 pounds

3. Dogs and cats do not live in the zoo. But many animals in the zoo eat dog or cat food. About how many pounds of dry dog and cat food combined do the zookeepers feed the animals each week?

   about 290 pounds

4. **What's Wrong?** Erica says that the zookeepers need about 100 bushels of apples to feed their animals for 2 weeks. What's wrong with her estimate?

   Answers may vary.

5. An adult's ticket to the San Diego Zoo costs $19.50. A child's ticket costs $11.75. About how much will it cost Mr. Jackson to buy a ticket for his daughter and himself?

   about $30.00

SAN DIEGO ZOO WEEKLY GROCERY LIST
33 pounds of dry cat food
43 bushels of apples
54 pounds of peanuts
66 pounds of sunflower seeds
112 dozen eggs
208 pounds of barley
259 pounds of dry dog food
279 ears of corn
471 papayas
875 pounds of bananas
948 heads of lettuce

Name ______________________ Date ____________

Problem Solving 4.3

Regroup Ones

Use Data Use the table to solve.

1. How many mammals in the United States are classified as threatened or endangered?

   74 mammals

2. How many threatened or endangered insects are there in the United States?

   44 insects

3. **Reasoning** Clams, snails, and crustaceans all have shells. One of these groups of animals has more than 50 endangered or threatened species in all. Which group is it?

   clams

4. **Write About It** Barry says that he does not need to regroup ones to find the total number of endangered or threatened fish in the United States. Do you agree? Explain why or why not.

   Yes; when you add the ones you get 5, which is less than 10. So you do not need to regroup the ones.

Threatened and Endangered Animals in the United States

Animal Group	Number Threatened	Number Endangered
Mammals	9	65
Birds	14	78
Reptiles	22	14
Amphibians	9	12
Fish	44	71
Clams	8	62
Snails	11	21
Insects	9	35
Arachnids	0	12
Crustaceans	3	18

Name ____________________ Date ____________

Problem Solving 4.4

Regroup Ones and Tens

Use the table to solve.

1. How much do an average male and an average female giant panda weigh altogether?

414 pounds

2. The sun bear is the smallest kind of bear in the world. How much do an average male and an average female sun bear weigh altogether?

163 pounds

3. **Reasoning** Ben found the combined average weight of the same kind of male and female bear. He had to regroup the ones, but not the tens, when he added. What kind of bear was it? What is the sum of their weights?

Asiatic black bear; 396 pounds

4. **What's Wrong?** Angie says that an average male and an average female American Black bear weigh 300 pounds together. Explain why Angie's sum is wrong.

Sample: Angie did not regroup when she added the tens.

Average Sizes of Bears

Type of Bear	Male Weight (in pounds)	Female Weight (in pounds)
Giant Panda	226	188
Asiatic Black	228	168
Sloth	243	165
Spectacled	225	160
Sun	85	78
American Black	250	150
Polar	1190	590

Name ______________________ Date ____________

Problem Solving 4.5

Problem-Solving Strategy: Guess and Check

Problem A caterpillar has twice as many legs as a spider has. Together, they have 24 legs. How many legs does the spider have? How many legs does the caterpillar have?

UNDERSTAND

1. Which bug has more legs? How do you know?

The caterpillar; It has twice as many legs as the spider.

PLAN

2. How will you check each of your guesses? Sample: I will find the sum of my guesses for each bug's number of legs and compare that sum to 24.

SOLVE

3. What is the solution to the problem?

The spider has 8 legs, and the caterpillar has 16 legs.

LOOK BACK

4. How can you check that your answers are reasonable?

Sample: I can check that my answers satisfy all of the facts given in the problem.

Name ________________________ Date ____________

Problem Solving 4.6

Column Addition

Answer each question about animals.

1. A greyhound can run 39 miles per hour. A gazelle can run 11 miles per hour faster than a greyhound. A cheetah can run 20 miles per hour faster than a gazelle. How fast can a cheetah run?

   70 miles per hour

   39+20+11=70

2. Most giraffes have a tail that is 36 inches long. A leopard's tail is usually 3 inches shorter than a giraffe's tail. An Asian elephant's tail is 5 inches longer than a leopard's tail. How long is the elephant's tail?

   38 inches

   36-3=33 33+5=38

   36-3

   33+5

3. California sea lion pups weigh about 16 pounds when they are born. The mother weighs about 160 pounds more than her pup. The father weighs about 485 pounds more than the mother. How much do adult male sea lions usually weigh?

   662 pounds

   Its incorrect.

   485 + 160 + 16 = 661

4. **Reasoning** Each beanbag animal at a toy store cost less than $10. Sara bought 3 of them for a total of $20. Two of the animals were the same price. The other cost $1 less. How much did each beanbag animal cost?

   Two beanbag animals cost $7, and one cost $6. 7+7+6=20

Name ______________________ Date ____________

Problem Solving 4.7

Add Greater Numbers

Use the table to solve.

1. How much do the Tiger Shark and the Black Marlin weigh altogether?

   3,340 pounds

   1,780+1,560=3340

2. Which two fish in the table weigh the least? What is their combined weight?

   Shortfin Mako Shark and swordfish; 2,403 pounds

3. Find the two fish in the table that weigh the most. How much do those two fish weigh altogether?

   4,444 pounds

   2,664+1,780=4,444

Largest Saltwater Fish Caught as of 2002	
Fish	**Weight**
Atlantic Blue Marlin	1,402 pounds
Black Marlin	1,560 pounds
Bluefin Tuna	1,496 pounds
Great White Shark	2,664 pounds
Greenland Shark	1,709 pounds
Pacific Blue Marlin	1,376 pounds
Shortfin Mako Shark	1,221 pounds
Swordfish	1,182 pounds
Tiger Shark	1,780 pounds

IGFA All-Tackle World Records

4. **What's Wrong?** Phil says that the swordfish and the Atlantic Blue Marlin together weigh more than a Great White Shark by itself. How can you show that Phil is wrong?

   1,182 + 1,402 = 2,584

   2,584 < 2,664

   1,182
   +1,402
   2,584

5. If someone catches a Tiger Shark that weighs 4,817 pounds more than the largest one caught before, then how much does this Tiger Shark weigh?

   6,597 pounds

   1,780
   +4,817
   6,597

Name ______________________ Date ____________

Choose a Method

Choose mental math, paper and pencil, or a calculator to solve each problem. Choices may vary.

1. The U.S. National Park System takes care of 56 national parks and 10 national seashores. How many national park sites is that in all?

   66 sites

2. The U.S. National Park System manages 75 national monuments and 28 national memorials. How many park sites is that in all?

   103 sites

3. Founded in 1872, Yellowstone National Park is our country's oldest national park. Shoshone National Forest is our country's oldest national forest. It was founded 19 years after Yellowstone. In what year was Shoshone National Forest founded?

   1891

4. Admission to Grand Canyon National Park is $20 per vehicle. A campsite can cost $25 per night. How much would it cost Olivia and her family to enter the park and spend 4 nights at the campsite?

   $120

Name ______________________ Date ____________

Problem Solving 4.9

Focus on Problem Solving
Estimate or Exact Answer

Problem Two giant pandas live in the National Zoo in Washington, D.C. Each panda eats about 40 pounds of bamboo every day. Is 200 pounds of bamboo enough to feed both pandas for two days?

UNDERSTAND

1. What does the word "enough" in the question tell you? *Sample:* It tells me that I need to know if the pandas need more or less than 200 pounds of bamboo.

PLAN

2. After you estimate, what do you need to do?
I need to compare my estimate to 200 pounds.

SOLVE

3. About how much food do they need for two days?
about 160 pounds

LOOK BACK

4. How could you rewrite the question so that it calls for an exact answer?
Sample: How much bamboo will the pandas eat in two days altogether?

Name ______________________ Date __________

Problem Solving 5.1

Subtraction Properties

Use subtraction properties to solve each problem.

Sports car: 1 passenger

Sedan: 3 passengers

Station Wagon: 5 passengers

Minivan: 7 passengers

Minibus: 15 passengers

1. Linda has a convertible sports car. After she picks up Ari, how many more passengers can she drive?

   0 passengers

2. If David is driving alone in his minivan, how many passenger seats in the minivan are empty?

   7 seats

3. **What's Wrong?** Toby says that the difference is 0 when zero is subtracted from the number of passengers a sports car can carry. What's wrong?

   Answers may vary.

   The sports cars can carry 1 passengers.

4. **Reasoning** When Mr. Chin drives his sons Paul, Lee, and Samuel to school, all of the passenger seats in his car are full. What kind of car does Mr. Chin drive?

   sedan

5. **Reasoning** The passengers from three kinds of vehicles filled all the passenger seats in the airport minibus. What are those three kinds of vehicles?

   sedan, station wagon, and minivan

Name ______________________ Date ____________

Problem Solving 5.2

Relate Addition and Subtraction

Answer each question. **Show your work.**

1. DeJuan is 8 years old. His sister is 12 years old. In how many years will DeJuan be the same age that his sister is now?

   4 years

2. **You Decide** Jonathan says that he can write a fact family for any three whole numbers. Do you think he can? Explain why or why not.

   No; *Explanations may vary.*

3. **Reasoning** We are two numbers in a fact family. We have a difference of 1 and a sum of 13. What numbers are we? How do you know?

   6 and 7; *Explanations may vary.*

4. **Write About It** Cynthia says that 25 subtracted from 48 is 23. How can she use addition to check her difference?

   She can add the difference and the number subtracted.

Name ________________________ Date ______________

Problem Solving 5.3

Estimate Differences

Use estimation to solve each problem.

Show your work.

1. The Wright brothers built and flew the first successful airplane in 1903. Their first flight lasted 12 seconds. Their longest flight was 59 seconds. About how much longer was their longest flight than their first flight?

   about 50 seconds

2. The Wright brothers' airplane was named *Flyer.* It was 253 inches long. It had a wingspan, or width, of 484 inches. About how much wider was the *Flyer* than it was long?

   about 200 inches

3. In 1927, Charles Lindbergh flew the first non-stop flight across the Atlantic Ocean. His plane, the *Spirit of St. Louis,* had a wingspan of 552 inches. About how much wider was the *Spirit of St. Louis* than the *Flyer?*

   about 100 inches

4. **Reasoning** The *Spirit of St. Louis* weighed 2,150 pounds. The *Flyer* weighed 1,545 pounds less than the *Spirit.* Explain why rounding these two numbers to the greatest place will not give a reasonable estimate for how much the *Flyer* weighed.

   Answers may vary.

5. Laura spent $14.87 on the two books shown below. About how much did *The Wright Brothers* book cost?

The Spirit of St. Louis
$8.79

The Wright Brothers

   about $6.00

Name ______________________ Date ____________

Problem Solving 5.4

Regroup Tens

Use the table to solve.

1. How many miles longer is New York's subway than Chicago's subway?

   434 miles

2. Which city's subway has more stations, Berlin or Mexico City? How many more stations?

   Berlin; 20 stations

3. In which two cities do the subways have about 150 stations? Which of those cities has the longer subway? How much longer?

   Mexico City and Tokyo; Tokyo; 72

4. Seoul is the capital of South Korea. Tokyo is the capital of Japan. Which of these Asian capital cities has the longer subway? How much longer?

   Tokyo; 99 miles

5. **Reasoning** If this city added 404 more miles to its subway, it would have the longest subway in the world. What city is it?

   London

World's Longest Subways

City	Number of Stations	Number of Miles
Berlin	170	90
Chicago	143	222
Copenhagen	22	14
London	275	253
Mexico City	150	111
Moscow	176	149
New York	468	656
Paris	368	124
Seoul	115	84
Tokyo	148	183

Show your work.

Name ______________________ Date ____________

Problem Solving 5.5

Regroup Tens and Hundreds

Chicago, Illinois, is one of the largest transportation centers in the United States. The table below shows the distances from Chicago to some other major cities in the United States. Use the table to solve each problem.

Driving Distances from Chicago	
City	**Number of Miles**
Atlanta	674
Boston	963
Dallas	917
Denver	996
Memphis	530
New Orleans	912
New York	802
Philadelphia	738
St. Louis	289
Washington, D.C.	671

Show your work.

1. Which city is farther from Chicago, Atlanta or Dallas? How much farther?

   Dallas; 243 miles

2. How many more miles is it from Chicago to New York than it is from Chicago to Philadelphia?

   64 miles

3. Which city in the table is closest to Chicago? Which city is farthest? What is the difference in the driving distances for those two cities?

   St. Louis; Denver;

   707 miles

4. Which city is closer to Chicago, Boston or Washington, D.C? How much closer?

   Washington, D.C.;

   292 miles

5. Brenda lives in New York. Her sister Phyllis lives in Atlanta. They both are driving to Chicago for a family reunion. Which sister will have to drive more miles to attend the reunion? How many more miles?

   Brenda; 128 miles

Name ______________________ Date __________

Problem Solving 5.6

Subtract Greater Numbers

Use the table to solve.

Shipping Fleets Around the World	
Country	**Number of Ships**
China	1,974
Germany	1,791
Greece	3,133
Japan	2,712
Norway	1,310
Russia	1,606
United States	1,521

* data from 2002

Show your work.

1. How many more ships does Japan have than China?

   738 ships

2. Which country listed in the table has the most ships? Which country has the fewest ships? What is the difference in the number of ships?

   Greece; Norway; 1,823 ships

3. Which country listed in the table has 368 fewer ships than China has?

   Russia

4. **What's Wrong?** Andrew says that the United States has 270 more ships than Germany has. What's wrong with Andrew's statement?

   He should have said that Germany has 270 more ships than the United States

5. **Write About It** Abby says that the United States and Russia have 3,127 ships altogether. How could you use subtraction to check if Abby is correct?

   Answers may vary.

6. Of all the ships in Greece, 1,345 are dry bulk carriers for shipping grains, sugar, and other loose materials. How many Greek ships are not dry bulk carriers?

   1,788 ships

Name ______________________ Date ____________

Problem Solving 5.7

Subtract Across Zeros

Solve each problem.

1. Maria's taxi ride downtown cost $5.68. She gave the driver $10.00. How much change did she get?

   $4.32

2. Mr. Diego is driving from Denver, Colorado, to Memphis, Tennessee, this weekend. The total distance is 1,040 miles. If he drives 650 miles on Saturday, how many miles will he have to drive on Sunday?

   390 miles

3. *Air Force One* can carry a total of 102 people. The plane always has a crew of 26 people. How many passengers can fly on *Air Force One* at the same time?

   76 passengers

4. **What's Wrong?** Harold did the subtraction shown at right. What did he do wrong?

   Answers may vary. He did not regroup the 10 tens as 9 tens and 10 ones before subtracting.

Harold

```
 3 10 10
  4̶0̶0̶
- 268
  142
```

Name ______________________ Date ____________

Problem Solving 5.8

Focus on Problem-Solving: Explain Your Answer

Problem A passenger helicopter can fly 150 miles per hour. If the helicopter is flying at 119 miles per hour, how much faster can it go? Explain.

1. What does the word "explain" mean in this problem?

It means that I have to tell how I found the answer and why I found it that way.

PLAN

2. What operation can you use to find your answer?

subtraction

SOLVE

3. Use words from the problem and math terms accurately to write your answer and explanation.

Answers may vary.

LOOK BACK

4. How can you check that your answer is reasonable?

Sample: I can use addition to check my subtraction: 31 + 119 = 150.

Use with text page 130.

Name ______________________ Date ____________

Problem Solving 6.1

Collect and Organize Data

Complete the tally chart below to record the information in the list.

Vote for Team Mascot		
Mascot	**Tally**	**Number**
Bulldog	||	2
Dolphin	|||	3
Lion	~~||||~~	5
Tiger	||	2

Our Choices for Our Team Mascot	
Kim	Dolphin
Phillip	Bulldog
Anita	Lion
Roy	Tiger
Allen	Dolphin
Melissa	Lion
Toby	Lion
Sheera	Tiger
Carlos	Bulldog
Mark	Lion
Caroline	Dolphin
Brent	Lion

1. How many team members were surveyed in all?

   12 team members

2. How many team members voted for a bulldog or a dolphin?

   5 team members

3. Which mascot got the most votes? How many team members did NOT vote for that mascot?

   lion;
   7 team members

4. **What's Wrong?** Roy says that the tiger got the fewest votes for the team's mascot. What's wrong?

   The tiger and the bulldog got the same number of votes.

5. **You Decide** Carlos recorded the number of votes for lions as |||||. Kim recorded those votes as ~~||||~~. Explain why they are both correct. Which method do you prefer? Why?

   Answers may vary.

6. **Write About It** Do you think it is easier to see which mascot got the most votes by looking at the list or by looking at the tally chart you made? Explain your thinking.

   Answers may vary.

Name ______________________ Date ____________

Problem Solving 6.2

Explore Range, Median, Mode, and Mean

The table below shows the number of teams playing each sport in the After-School Sports League. Use snap cubes to show this information. Then use the cubes to answer each question.

After-School Sports League	
Sport	**Number of Teams**
Basketball	9
Hockey	5
Soccer	9
Baseball	10
Football	7

Show your work.

1. What is the median of the data set? Explain how you rearranged the stacks to find your answer.

   9; Explanations may vary.

2. What is the range of the data set?

   5

3. What is the mean number of teams that play each sport in the After-School Sports League? What did you do to each stack of cubes to find your answer?

   8; Explanations may vary.

4. **What's Wrong?** Bryant says that the median number of teams that play each sport is 9, because more sports in the league have 9 teams than any other number. What's wrong?

   Answers may vary.

5. **What If?** If another basketball team joined the league, would the range, median, or mode of the data set change? Explain your answers.

   The mode would change; the range and median would not.

Name ______________________ Date ____________

Problem Solving 6.3

Line Plots

The line plot below shows the number of touchdowns that were scored in each Super Bowl game from 1990 to 2002. Use the line plot to answer Questions 1–5.

Touchdowns Scored in Super Bowl Games

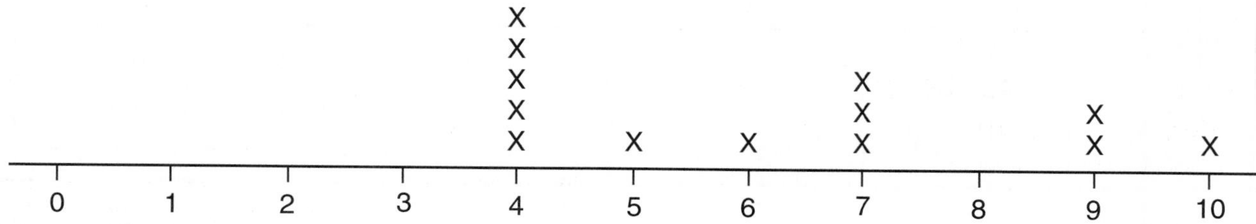

1. In how many of the Super Bowls were exactly 5 touchdowns scored?

   1 Super Bowl

2. In how many of the games were more than 7 touchdowns scored?

   3 games

3. The 1995 Super Bowl had the greatest number of touchdowns. How many touchdowns were scored during that game?

   10 touchdowns

4. What are the range and mode for this Super Bowl data set?

   Range: 6 touchdowns; Mode: 4 touchdowns

5. **What If?** There were 3 touchdowns scored in the 1989 Super Bowl. If this data is added to the line plot, will the range or the mode of the data set change? Explain.

   Explanations may vary; The range changes, the mode does not

Name ______________________ Date ____________

Problem Solving 6.4

Problem-Solving Strategy: Make a Table

Problem The Sport Zone sells packages that contain 2 golf balls and 5 golf tees. George bought enough packages to have 30 golf tees. How many golf balls did he get?

UNDERSTAND

1. What do you want to know?

how many golf balls George got

PLAN

2. How many columns should your table have? What should their labels be?

2 columns; Number of Golf Balls; Number of Golf Tees

SOLVE

3. Make your table. What is the solution to the problem?

Check students' tables; George got 12 golf balls.

Number of Golf Balls	Number of Golf Tees
2	5
4	10
6	15
8	20
10	25
12	30

4. How many packages did George buy? How can you use this fact to check that your answer is reasonable?

6 packages; $6 \times 2 = 12$ and $6 \times 5 = 30$. So, my answer is reasonable.

Name ______________________ Date ____________

Problem Solving 6.5

Make a Pictograph

The table below shows the number of gold medals that each of the top four countries won at the 2000 Summer Olympic Games held in Sydney, Australia.

Olympic Gold Medals Won	
Country	**Number of Medals**
Australia	16
China	28
Russia	32
United States	40

1. **Represent** Make a pictograph of the data in the table. Use this key: Each stands for 4 gold medals won.

Olympic Gold Medals Won	
Country	Number of Medals
Australia	
China	
Russia	
United States	

Key: Each stands for 4 gold medals.

Use your pictograph to answer Questions 2–5

2. How many pictures did you draw for China in your pictograph? Why?

   7 pictures; $28 \div 4 = 7$

3. For which country did you draw the most pictures? Why?

   United States; It won the most gold medals.

4. **You Decide** Why is 4 a good choice for the number of gold medals that each stands for in the pictograph?

   All of the data in the table evenly divides by 4.

5. **Reasoning** Germany won 14 gold medals in the 2000 Summer Olympics. How would you display this data on the pictograph?

   3 whole pictures and 1 half picture

Name ______________________ Date ____________

Problem Solving 6.6

Make a Bar Graph

1. The table at right shows the number of games some NBA basketball teams won in the 2000–2001 season. Use the grid at left to make a vertical or horizontal bar graph of the data in this table. Use a scale of 5.

NBA Game Wins, 2000–2001

Team	Number of Games
Atlanta	25
Chicago	15
Denver	40
Houston	45
Miami	50

Check students' bar graphs.

Use the bar graph to answer each question.

2. What title and labels did you use for your graph?

Title: NBA Game Wins, 2000–2001; labels: Team; Number of Games

3. What is the greatest number on your scale? What is the least number?

greatest number: 50; least number: 0

4. Which bar on your graph is the shortest? Why?

Chicago, because Chicago won the fewest games.

5. Which team won half as many games as Miami won? How can you tell from your graph?

Atlanta; Miami's bar is twice as long as Atlanta's bar.

Name ______________________ Date ____________

Problem Solving 6.7

Read Graphs with Ordered Pairs

The grid below shows the locations of different places along a triathlon race route. Use the grid to solve each problem.

Water Station B (6, 9)
Running Station (2, 8)
Finish Line (8, 7)
Water Station A (3, 5)
First Aid Station (6, 5)
Awards Stage (9, 5)
Bike Station (5, 3)
Starting Line (1, 2)
Parking Lot (3, 2)

1. The competitors swim 2 miles to the place located at (5, 3) on the grid. What is that place?

   Bike Station

2. Donna volunteered to work at a water station during the race. Which two ordered pairs could give her location on the grid?

   (3, 5) or (6, 9)

3. **Reasoning** The second number in the ordered pair for this place on the grid is the same as the second number in the ordered pair for the First Aid Station. It is not a water station. What place is it?

   Awards Stage

4. **What's Wrong?** Peter says the race ends at (7, 8) on the grid. What mistake did he make?

   He reversed the ordered pair. He should have said (8, 7).

5. The race planners want to add another first aid station located 2 spaces to the right and 1 unit up from the Running Station on the grid. What ordered pair gives the location of this new first aid station?

   (4, 9)

Name ______________________ Date ____________

Problem Solving 7.1

Understand Probability

Use the spinner at right to answer Questions 1–5.

Red, Yellow, Red, Green, Red, Green

1. On which color is the spinner likely to land? Why?

   Red; most of the spinner is colored red.

2. **Write About It** You spin the spinner once. Describe a certain event. Explain why you can describe your event that way.

   The spinner will land on red, green, or yellow. This event is certain because those are the only colors on the spinner.

3. **You Decide** Why is it possible, but unlikely, that the spinner will land on green?

   It is possible because green is on the spinner. It is unlikely because green covers less than half the spinner.

4. **Reasoning** If you know that an event is likely or unlikely, what other word can you use to describe the event? Explain how you know.

   Possible; if an event is likely or unlikely, it must also be possible.

5. **Reasoning** How could you change the spinner to make it impossible to land on yellow?

   Make the yellow section a different color.

Name ____________________ Date ____________

Problem Solving 7.2

Identify Outcomes

Use the spinner at right to answer Questions 1–3.

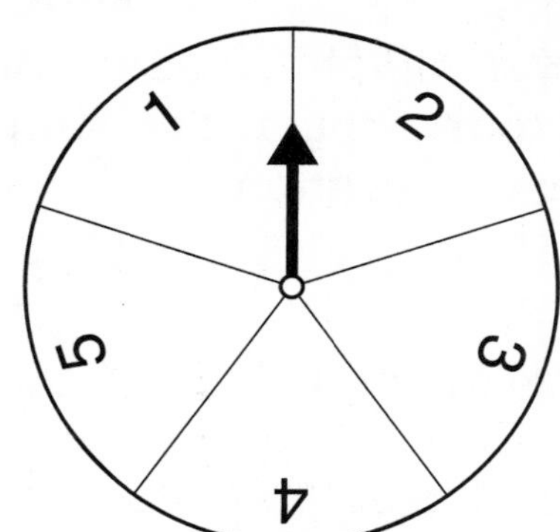

1. How many possible outcomes are there for each spin? What are those outcomes?

   5 possible outcomes; 1, 2, 3, 4, or 5

2. **Reasoning** You spin the spinner twice. The sum of both spins' numbers is one outcome. How could you find all the possible outcomes?

   I could make an organized list to find all the possible sums of two numbers from 1 to 5.

Kendra has two of the spinners shown above. She spins both spinners 100 times. Each time, she records the sum of the two spins' numbers. The results of her experiment are recorded in the table below. Use the table to answer Questions 3–4.

3. How many possible outcomes are there? Why is 1 NOT a possible outcome for the experiment?

   9 possible outcomes; The least sum possible is 1 + 1 = 2.

Spinning Two Spinners

Outcome	2	3	4	5	6	7	8	9	10
Number of Occurrences	4	7	10	15	23	17	11	8	5

4. **You Decide** Which outcome occurred most often in Kendra's experiment? Why do you think this outcome occurred most often?

   A sum of 6; There are more ways to get a sum of 6 from two numbers from 1 to 5 than any other sum.

Name ______________________ Date ______________

Problem Solving 7.3

Outcomes and Probability

Some friends are playing a probability game with the letters shown below. The cards will be placed in a bag. Each player will pick a card without looking. The card is returned to the bag after each pick. Use the cards to answer each question.

P	R	O	B	A	B	I	L	I	T	Y

1. What is the probability of picking a P from the bag?

   1 out of 11

2. Rob wants to know the probability of picking any letter in his name. What is the probability?

   4 out of 11

3. **Reasoning** The chances of picking this letter are the same as picking a B. What letter is it? How do you know?

   I; There are the same number of I's in the bag as there are B's.

4. **What if?** Suppose the letter Y was not in the bag. Would the probability of picking an R change? Why or why not?

   Yes; The number of possible outcomes would change to 10 instead of 11.

5. **What's Wrong?** Mary says the probability of picking the letter T is 1. What's wrong?

   The probability is 1 out of 11.

Use with text pages 182–183.

Name ______________________ Date ____________

Problem Solving 7.4

Make Predictions

Rita spun a spinner 30 times and recorded the results on the bar graph below. Use the graph to answer Questions 1–3.

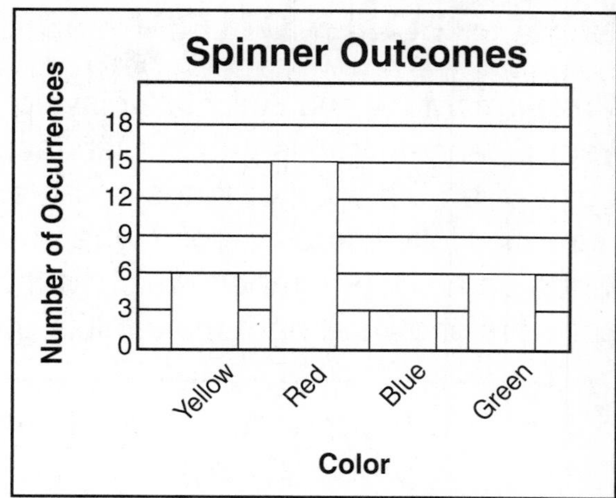

1. How many times did she spin yellow?

   6 times

2. **Write About It** What is a likely prediction for the color she will spin next? Explain your thinking.

   Red; Her experiment resulted in the most red spins. So, the probability of landing on red is more likely.

3. **Represent** On a separate page, draw and color an example of a spinner that probably looks like the spinner Rita used in her experiment.

   Check students' drawings.

4. **Reasoning** A bag has 10 tennis balls that are three different colors. Chaz picks a ball from the bag 40 times without looking and returns it to the bag each time. The results of his experiment are 4 pink, 21 yellow, and 15 purple. How many of each color ball do you think are in the bag? Explain your answers.

   There are 5 yellow balls, 4 purple balls, and 1 pink ball. Explanations will vary.

Name ________________________ Date ____________

Problem-Solving Application: Use Probability

Problem Mark and Holly are playing Take Your Chances. In this game, Mark scores a point when the spinner lands on an even number. Holly scores a point when the spinner lands on an odd number. Which of the spinners shown at right makes this game fair?

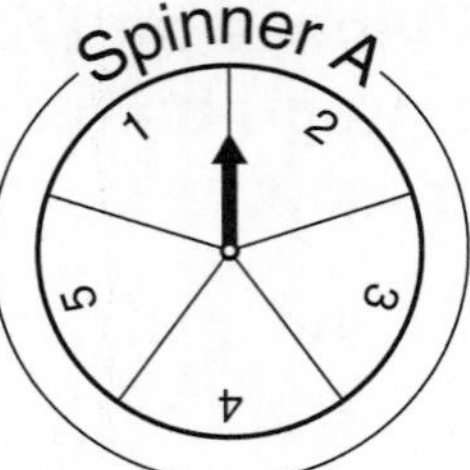

UNDERSTAND

1. Do you have all the information you need to solve the problem? Explain.

Yes; I know the rules for the game, and see the spinners.

PLAN

2. When is a game fair? When all players have an equal chance to win

SOLVE

3. Which spinner makes the game fair? Explain your choice.

Spinner B; With Spinner B, both players have 3 out of 6 chances of scoring a point.

LOOK BACK

4. How could you change the unfair spinner so that the game is fair with both spinners?

Add a section labeled 6 to Spinner A.

Name ______________________ Date ____________

Model Multiplication as Repeated Addition

Solve each problem.

1. Fill in the blanks to describe the dolls in John's collection shown below.

__3__ groups of __2__ dolls

2. **You Decide** Toni buys 8 identical packs of comic books for his collection. What must you know before you can multiply to find the total number of comic books Toni bought?

how many comic books there are in each pack

3. Sally has 4 brown bears, 4 black bears, and 4 gray bears in her stuffed bear collection. How can you add to find Sally's total number of bears? What multiplication sentence will give you the same total?

Add three fours: $4 + 4 + 4 = 12$; $3 \times 4 = 12$

4. **What's Wrong** Jessica has 4 groups of 4 rocks in her rock collection. She says she has 8 rocks in her collection altogether. What's wrong?

She added $4 + 4$ instead of multiplying 4×4. She has 16 rocks, not 8 rocks.

Name ______________________ Date ______________

Problem Solving 8.2

Arrays and Multiplication

Use the stickers at right to solve Problems 1–5.

1. Fill in the blanks to describe the sheet of stickers.

   6 rows of 5 stickers

2. Multiply to find the total number of stickers that are on the sheet.

   $6 \times 5 = 30$ or $5 \times 6 = 30$

3. **Reasoning** How can you use addition to check your product in Problem 2?

   I can add five 6s: $6 + 6 + 6 + 6 + 6 = 30$.

Solve each problem.

4. **Reading** Marcos buys a sheet of stickers that has 3 rows of stickers. Each row has the same number of stickers. After he takes one of the stickers off, there are 20 stickers left on the sheet. How many stickers were in each row of the sheet Marcos bought? Explain how you know.

   7 stickers in each row;
   Explanations may vary.

5. **Reasoning** A checkerboard has 8 rows of 8 squares. Half of the squares are black. How many squares on the checkerboard are black? Explain.

   32; *Explanations may vary.*

Name ______________________ Date ____________

Problem Solving 8.3

Multiply With 2

Use the table to solve each problem.

Party Favors Package	
Party Favor	**Number in Each Package**
Beach Balls	2
Balloons	9
Trading Cards	6
Stickers	8
Kazoos	5
Tattoos	7
Noise Makers	3
Bubble Makers	4

1. Tanya buys two packages of balloons for her birthday party. How many balloons does she buy in all?

   18 balloons

2. Vince used two packages of kazoos to make party favor bags for his party. He put one kazoo in each bag and gave one bag to each guest. How many guests came to Vince's party?

   10 guests

3. **Reasoning** Felicia buys two packages of a party favor. She now has 12 of those items in all. Which party favor did Felicia buy?

   trading cards

4. A package of tattoos costs $3. A package of stickers costs $4. Steve buys two packages of each. How much money does he spend in all?

   $14

5. **What's Wrong?** Larry says that one package of balloons has twice as many party favors as one package of bubble makers. What's wrong?

   Answers may vary.

Name ______________________ Date ______________

Problem Solving 8.4

Multiply With 4

Yang collects stamps from countries in South America. He made the pictograph below to show his collection. Use the pictograph to solve each problem.

Yang's Stamp Collection

Country	Number of Stamps
Argentina	[stamp] [stamp] [stamp] [stamp] [stamp] [stamp]
Bolivia	[stamp] [stamp] [stamp]
Brazil	[stamp] [stamp] [stamp] [stamp] [stamp] [stamp] [stamp] [stamp] [stamp]
Chile	[stamp] [stamp] [stamp] [stamp] [stamp] [stamp] [stamp] [stamp]
Colombia	[stamp] [stamp] [stamp] [stamp] [stamp]
Ecuador	[stamp] [stamp]
Peru	[stamp] [stamp] [stamp] [stamp]
Venezuela	[stamp] [stamp] [stamp] [stamp] [stamp] [stamp] [stamp]

Each [stamp] stands for 4 stamps

1. How many stamps does Yang have from Argentina?

   24 stamps

2. How many stamps in Yang's collection are from Venezuela?

   28 stamps

3. From which country does Yang have the most stamps? How many of those stamps does he have?

   Brazil; 36 stamps

4. **What's Wrong?** Yang's sister Hyun looks at his pictograph and says that Yang has 8 stamps from Chile in his collection. What mistake did Hyun make?

   Answers may vary.

Name ______________________ Date ____________

Problem Solving 8.5

Multiply With 5

Solve each problem.

1. Kojo has the coins shown at right. Write two different multiplication sentences to find the total amount of money Kojo has.

   5 × 6 = 30 or 6 × 5 = 30; He has 30¢.

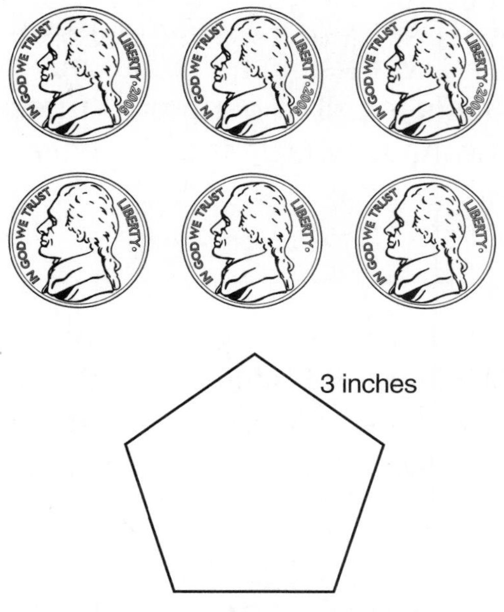

2. A pentagon has 5 sides. All the sides of a regular pentagon have the same length. What is the total distance around the regular pentagon at the right?

   15 inches

Tessa
5 × 27 = 134
5 × 39 = 195
5 × 42 = 208
5 × 51 = 251

3. **You Decide** Tessa wrote the multiplication sentences shown at the right. Without multiplying, how can you tell which of Tessa's multiplication sentences is correct?

   5 × 39 = 195 is correct, because the product of 5 and any other factor has a 5 or a 0 in the ones place.

4. **Reasoning** What is the greatest possible product you get when you multiply 5 by a one-digit number?

   45

Name ____________________ Date ____________

Problem Solving 8.6

Multiply With 10

Solve each problem.

1. Each of Cheryl's 10 model trucks has 6 wheels. If she has to buy new wheels for all of her model trucks, how many wheels will she have to buy?

   60 wheels

2. Tori displays her model train collection on 5 shelves. Each shelf holds 10 trains. How many trains does Tori have in her collection?

   50 trains

3. David's remote-control airplane can fly 10 miles per hour. If David flew the plane for 3 hours, how many miles did the plane fly?

   30 miles

4. A model car kit costs $10.00. A model sailboat kit costs twice as much as a model car kit. How much does the model sailboat kit cost?

   $20.00

5. **Reasoning** What is the least possible product when you multiply 10 by a two-digit number? Explain how you know.

   100, because 10 is the least two-digit number, and 10 × 10 = 100.

Name ______________________ Date ____________

Problem Solving 8.7

Problem-Solving Strategy: Make an Organized List

Problem Jan's favorite video game in his collection is *Fast Track.* To play it, he must choose a car, a truck, or a motorcycle to drive. He also has to pick the color for the vehicle—red, blue, green, or black. How many different combinations can Jan choose?

UNDERSTAND

1. What will be combined in each choice?

a vehicle and a color

PLAN

2. If you start with a car, how will you make your organized list?

Sample answer: First I will match the car with each color choice. Then I will do the same thing with the truck and with the motorcycle.

SOLVE

3. How can you check that you did not miss or repeat any combinations in your list?

Answers may vary.

4. How many different combinations can Jan choose? ____________

12 different combinations

LOOK BACK

5. Why is car → truck NOT a possible combination?

Answers may vary. Sample: Each combination must be a vehicle and a color, not a vehicle and a vehicle.

Name ______________________ Date ____________

Problem Solving 8.8

Multiply With 1 and 0

Solve each problem.

1. Dan has the frames shown at right to display his autograph collection. What two multiplication sentences show the total number of autographs displayed now?

   $3 \times 0 = 0$ and $0 \times 3 = 0$

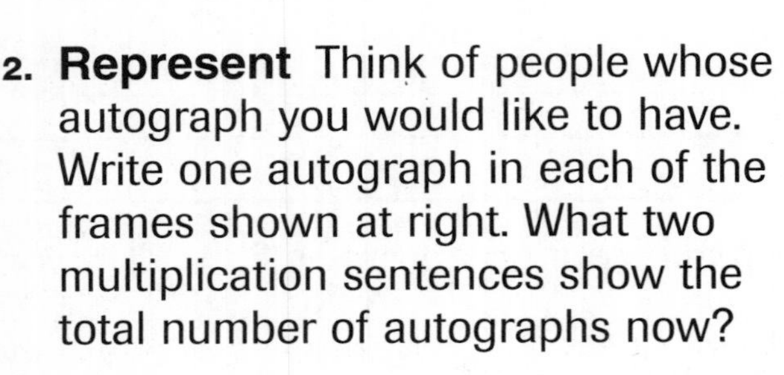

2. **Represent** Think of people whose autograph you would like to have. Write one autograph in each of the frames shown at right. What two multiplication sentences show the total number of autographs now?

   $3 \times 1 = 3$ and $1 \times 3 = 3$

3. **Reasoning** What is the least possible product when you multiply 1 by a one-digit number? Explain.

   0; because 0 is the least one-digit number and $1 \times 0 = 0$.

4. **What's Wrong?** Kirk says that the product of 1 and any number has a 1 in the ones place. What's wrong?

   Sample answer: The product can end in any digit, depending on what number is multiplied by 1.

Name ______________________ Date ____________

Problem Solving 9.1

Patterns on a Multiplication Table

Use the multiplication table at right to solve each problem.

1. Fill in all the missing products in the multiplication table.

   Check students' tables.

2. Which row has the same numbers as the column for 10?

   row for 10

3. In which rows do all the numbers end in a 5 or a 0?

   5 and 10

4. **Reasoning** Which row and column have the same number written in every square?

   row for 0 and column for 0

×	0	1	2	3	4	5	6	7	8	9	10
0				0			0	0	0	0	
1				3			6	7	8	9	
2				6			12	14	16	18	
3	0	3	6	9	12	15	18	21	24	27	30
4				12			24	28	32	36	
5				15			30	35	40	45	
6	0	6	12	18	24	30	36	42	48	54	60
7	0	7	14	21	28	35	42	49	56	63	70
8	0	8	16	24	32	40	48	56	64	72	80
9	0	9	18	27	36	45	54	63	72	81	90
10				30			60	70	80	90	

Represented below are parts of a multiplication table. Which row or column is shown? Fill in the missing products for each.

5.

	12		
12	16	20	24
		25	

rows for 3 to 5; columns for 3 to 6

6.

48	56	64	72
54			81

rows for 8 and 9; columns for 6 to 9

Name ______________________ Date ____________

Problem Solving 9.2

Multiply With 3

1. There are 3 groups of hikers in the Rain Forest Hiking Club. There are 7 hikers in each group. Draw arrows on the number line below to skip count by 3s to find the total number of hikers in the club.

21

Solve each problem.

2. **Represent** Shari is making a pictograph to show the number of people in each of her club's hiking groups. On her graph, one 🚶 stands for 3 people. How many pictures should she draw to show a group of 18 hikers?

6 pictures

3. **Predict** In May, the club members hiked 3 miles each weekend. In June, they hiked 6 miles each weekend. In July, they hiked 12 miles each weekend. If this pattern continues, how many miles are the club members likely to hike each weekend in August?

24 miles

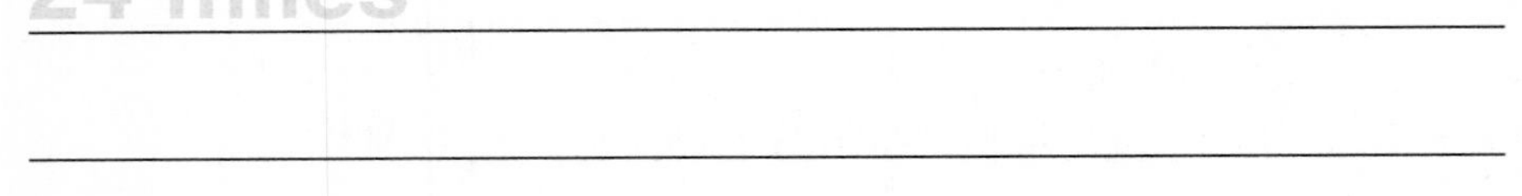

4. **Reasoning** Both of my factors are the same number. My product is 9. What are my two factors?

3 and 3

Name ______________________ Date ____________

Problem Solving 9.3

Multiply With 6

Solve each problem about rain forest animals.

1. You can recognize a toucan in the rain forest by its long, colorful beak. A toucan's beak is usually 6 inches long. Its body is usually 3 times longer than its beak. How long is the toucan's body?

   18 inches

2. Leafcutter ants chew up leaves in rain forests to get their favorite food–fungus! A leafcutter ant has 6 legs. How many legs do 9 leafcutter ants have in all?

   54 legs

3. Howler monkeys live in the canopy, or treetops, of rain forests. They often live in small groups. If there are 6 howler monkeys in a group, how many are in 4 groups?

   24 monkeys

4. **Reasoning** Green anoles and green iguanas are two rainforest lizards. Green anoles are about 6 inches long. Green iguanas are 10 times as long as green anoles. How can finding 3×10 help you find the length of a green iguana?

   $3 \times 10 = 30$, and $30 + 30 = 60$.
   So, $6 \times 10 = 60$.

Name ______________________ Date ____________

Problem Solving 9.4

Multiply With 7

Solve each problem about rainforest plants.

1. Many plants grow in rain forests because of the very rainy climates. In fact, most rain forests receive at least 7 inches of rain each month. How many inches of rain do most rain forests get in 4 months?

   28 inches

2. Bromeliads are one kind of plant that lives in rain forests. Their large curved leaves form a bowl shape to collect water. Some bromeliads can hold 2 gallons of water. How much water can 7 bromeliads hold altogether?

   14 gallons

3. The petroleum nut tree grows in Asian rain forests. Its seeds contain oil, which is burned as fuel. One petroleum nut tree produces 3 tablespoons of oil each day. How much oil does one petroleum nut tree produce each week?

   21 tablespoons

4. **Reasoning** About 1,000 trees in rain forests are cut down every minute! How could you use repeated addition to find how many trees are cut down in 7 minutes?

   Add 1,000 seven times: 1,000 + 1,000 + 1,000 + 1,000 + 1,000 + 1,000 + 1,000 = 7,000

Name ____________________ Date ____________

Problem Solving 9.5

Multiply With 8

The students at Franklin Elementary School collected newspapers for recycling. The pictograph at right shows how many pounds of newspaper each grade collected. Use the pictograph to solve Problems 1–4.

Paper Collected for Recycling

Grade	Pounds of Newspaper
First Grade	4 symbols
Second Grade	6 symbols
Third Grade	9 symbols
Fourth Grade	5 symbols
Fifth Grade	8 symbols

Each symbol stands for 8 pounds of newspaper.

1. How many pounds of newspaper did the fifth-graders collect?

   64 pounds

2. Which grade collected the most newspaper? How many pounds did that grade collect?

   third grade; 72 pounds

3. Which grade collected more newspaper, the second grade or the fourth grade? How much more?

   second grade; 8 pounds more

4. In the United States, an average family of 4 people uses a total of 8 pounds of paper every day! How many pounds of paper is that every week?

   56 pounds

Name ______________________ Date ______________

Problem Solving 9.6

Multiply With 9

Solve each problem about foods from rain forests.

1. Cashews, Brazil nuts, and peanuts originally grew in rain forests. Anne made a trail mix with 9 cups of each. How many cups of cashews, Brazil nuts, and peanuts did she use in all?

   27 cups

2. Yams also grow in rain forests. Connie cooked 9 yams for Thanksgiving dinner. Her friend Crystal cooked twice as many yams. How many yams did Crystal cook?

   18 yams

3. Chocolate comes from the rain forest cocoa plant. One ounce of milk chocolate contains 9 grams of fat. How many grams of fat are in a 6-ounce milk chocolate bar?

   54 grams

4. Vanilla comes from the seed of rain forest orchids. The seeds grow in long thin pods. Ten workers harvest 9 orchids each. How many orchids did the workers harvest?

   90 orchids

5. **Reasoning** Rain forests gave us oranges, too. One slice of an orange contains 9 milligrams of Vitamin C. Doctors recommend that children consume 45 milligrams of Vitamin C each day. How many slices of oranges should you eat to get the Vitamin C you need each day?

   5 slices

Name ______________________ Date ____________

Problem Solving 9.7

Patterns on a Multiplication Table

Use the multiplication table at right to solve each problem.

×	0	1	2	3	4	5	6	7	8	9	10	11	12
0	0	0	0	0	0	0	0	0	0	0	0	0	0
1	0	1	2	3	4	5	6	7	8	9	10	11	12
2	0	2	4	6	8	10	12	14	16	18	20	22	24
3	0	3	6	9	12	15	18	21	24	27	30	33	36
4	0	4	8	12	16	20	24	28	32	36	40	44	48
5	0	5	10	15	20	25	30	35	40	45	50	55	60
6	0	6	12	18	24	30	36	42	48	54	60	66	72
7	0	7	14	21	28	35	42	49	56	63	70	77	84
8	0	8	16	24	32	40	48	56	64	72	80	88	96
9	0	9	18	27	36	45	54	63	72	81	90	99	108
10	0	10	20	30	40	50	60	70	80	90	100	110	120
11	0	11	22	33	44	55	66	77	88	99	110	121	132
12	0	12	24	36	48	60	72	84	96	108	120	132	144

1. **Reasoning** One of my multiples is 24. I am a multiple of six numbers in the table. What number am I?

   12

2. **Reasoning** I am a square number. I am an odd two-digit number. The sum of my digits is a two-digit number. What number am I?

   49

3. **Write About It** If you know that a multiple is even, what do you know about its two factors?

   If the multiple is even, then at least one of its factors is even.

4. **You Decide** Phyllis says that any multiple of 6 is also a multiple of 2. Aaron says that any multiple of 6 is also a multiple of 3. Who do you think is right? Explain.

   They are both right; $2 \times 3 = 6$, so any multiple of 6 is also a multiple of 2 and 3.

5. **What's Wrong?** Keesha says that the product of 9 and any number is twice the product of 3 and that number. What's wrong?

   Answers may vary

Name ______________________ Date ____________

Problem Solving 9.8

Multiply Three Numbers

Solve each problem.

1. Jim, Angie, and Ryan each made 2 rain forest picture books. They drew 5 pictures in each book. How many pictures did they draw in all?

   30 pictures

2. Diego bought 7 sheets of rain forest stickers. Each sheet had 3 rows of 4 stickers. How many stickers did he buy in all?

   84 stickers

3. Pairs of students are giving reports on rain forests. Each student will give a 6-minute report. There are 8 pairs of students. What is the total amount of time needed for all the reports?

   96 minutes

4. For homework, each student will find 4 facts each about 2 rain forest animals. If 11 students are doing the homework assignment, how many facts will they collect in all?

   88 facts

5. **Reasoning** Alex found the product of 5, 2, and one other number. The product was 80. What was the other number? How do you know?

   8, because $5 \times 2 =$
   10 and $10 \times 8 = 80$

Name ______________________ Date __________

Problem Solving 9.9

Problem-Solving Decision: Multistep Problems

Problem Most anteaters live in South American rainforests. There are 3 main kinds of anteaters. The smallest is the silky anteater. It is 12 inches long. The largest is the giant anteater. It is 6 times as long as the silky anteater. What is the difference in these two anteaters' lengths?

1. What does the word "difference" mean in the problem?

   It means you need to subtract.

PLAN

2. Write the two steps and operations needed to solve the problem in the order you will do them.

   Step 1: Find the length of the giant anteater; multiply.

   Step 2: Find the difference in their lengths; subtract.

SOLVE

3. What is the answer to the problem? 60 inches

LOOK BACK

4. Could you have done your steps in a different order and still solved the problem?

   Explain. No; explanations may vary.

Name ______________________ Date ____________

The Meaning of Division

Solve each problem.

Show your work.

1. **Represent** Ben has 15 counters. To divide them into equal groups, Ben draws the circles below. Draw dots to show the number of counters Ben should place in each circle.

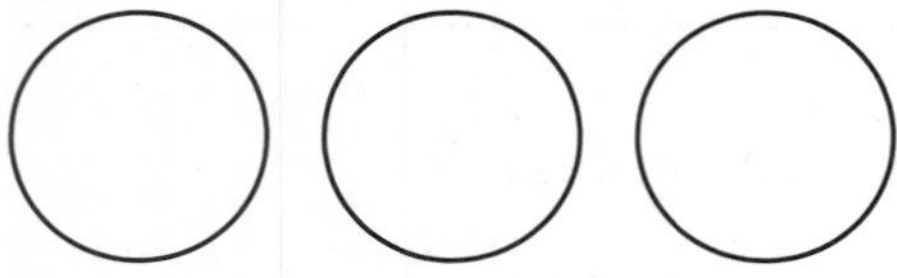

Check students' drawings. Drawings should show 5 dots in each circle.

2. Write a division sentence to describe your completed picture from Problem 1. Label each part of the sentence as *number of counters, number of groups,* or *number in each group.*

15 ÷ 3 = 5 with labels: 15 = number of counters
3 = number of groups, 5 = number in each grou

3. **Reasoning** Sarah and Cal each have 12 counters. Sarah places an equal number of her counters in each of 3 circles. Cal places an equal number of his counters in each of 4 circles. Whose circles have more counters in each circle?

Sarah's

4. **Reasoning** Latifa has 8 counters. Steve has twice as many counters as Latifa. They combine their counters and then share them equally. How many counters do they each get?

12 counters

Name ______________________ Date ______________

Problem Solving 10.2

Model Division as Repeated Subtraction

Solve each problem. **Show your work.**

1. Phil wants to use repeated subtraction to find 18 ÷ 6. At what number should he start counting back? At what number should he stop counting back?

   18; 0

2. In Problem 1, by what number should Phil count back? What will the number of times he counts back tell him?

   by 6s; the quotient of 18 ÷ 6

3. **What's Wrong?** Look at Candice's work at right. What mistake did she make when she used repeated subtraction to divide?

   She did not count the number of times she subtracted. 20 ÷ 4 = 5.

Candice
Find 20 ÷ 4.
20 − 4 = 16
16 − 4 = 12
12 − 4 = 8
8 − 4 = 4
4 − 4 = 0
So, 20 ÷ 4 = 0

4. **Write About It** How is using repeated subtraction to divide like using repeated addition to multiply?

   Answers may vary.

Name ______________________ Date ____________

Problem Solving 10.3

Relate Multiplication and Division

Answer each question.

1. Fill in the blanks to describe with multiplication this sheet of animal stickers.

2 × 5 = 10

number of rows of stickers	×	number of stickers in each row	=	total number of stickers
2	×	5	=	10

2. Fill in the blanks to describe the same sheet of animal stickers with division in two ways.

total number of stickers	÷	number of rows of stickers	=	number of stickers in each row
10	÷	2	=	5

total number of stickers	÷	number of stickers in each row	=	number of rows of stickers
10	÷	5	=	2

3. Write 4 different multiplication and division sentences using the numbers 3, 9, and 27.

3 × 9 = 27

9 × 3 = 27

27 ÷ 3 = 9

27 ÷ 9 = 3

4. Reasoning If an array shows a square number, how many multiplication and division sentences can describe the array?

2 sentences

Use with text pages 264–265.

Name ______________________ Date ____________

Problem Solving 10.4

Divide by 2

At Paw's Pet Store, 2 animals share each cage. The table below shows how many animals are in the store now. Use the table to solve each problem.

Paw's Pet Store Animals	
Animal	**Number**
Mice	22
Snakes	4
Hamsters	18
Cats	12
Birds	16
Guinea Pigs	10
Rabbits	14
Lizards	6
Crickets	20
Dogs	8

1. How many cages are needed for all the birds?

   8 cages

2. How many cages are needed for all the rabbits?

   7 cages

3. How many more cages are needed to hold all the hamsters than to hold all the guinea pigs?

   4 more cages

4. Which kind of animal needs twice as many cages as all the lizards need?

   cat

5. **Reasoning** The pet store uses a total of 6 cages to hold two different kinds of animals. What animals are they?

   snakes and dogs

Name ______________________ Date ______________

Problem Solving 10.5

Problem-Solving Decision: Choose the Operation

Problem Each minibus seats 6 passengers. There are 30 third-graders going on the field trip to the petting zoo. How many minibuses are needed to drive all the students?

UNDERSTAND

1. What do you want to know?

the number of minibuses needed to drive all the students

PLAN

2. Do you need to combine the groups or separate the groups? What operation will you use?

separate groups; division

SOLVE

3. Write your solution in a complete sentence.

Five minibuses are needed to drive all the students.

LOOK BACK

4. Could you have used a different operation to solve the problem? Explain.

Yes; I could use repeated subtraction.

Name ______________________ Date ____________

Problem Solving 10.6

Divide by 5

Display the data given in the table at left on the pictograph at right.

Then use your completed pictograph to solve each problem.

Dog Show Competitors	
Dog Breed	**Number of Dogs**
Poodle	35
German Shepherd	10
Beagle	15
Retriever	20
Terrier	45

Dog Show Competitors

Dog Breed	Number of Dogs
Poodle	7 bones
German Shepherd	2 bones
Beagle	3 bones
Retriever	4 bones
Terrier	9 bones

Each bone stands for 5 dogs

1. How many pictures did you draw for poodles? Why that many?

   7 pictures, because each picture stands for 5 dogs and $35 \div 5 = 7$

2. For which dog breed did you draw 4 pictures? Why that many?

   retriever, $20 \div 5 = 4$

3. **What's Wrong?** Kylie drew 5 pictures for German shepherds on her pictograph because $5 + 5 = 10$.

   She should have drawn 2 pictures.

4. **Represent** Last year, there were twice as many beagles competing in the dog show. How would you show that number of beagles on the pictograph? Explain.

   6 pictures; $15 \times 2 = 30$ and $30 \div 5 = 6$.

Show your work.

Name ______________________ Date ______________

Problem Solving 10.7

Divide by 10

Use the sign to solve each problem.

1. Last month, Carolyn spent a total of $50 on riding lessons. How many lessons did she take?

   5 lessons

2. Chandra spent a total of $30 riding at Giddy-Up Horse Farm. How many hours did she ride?

   3 hours

3. **Reasoning** Devon paid the exact cost of his riding lessons with 2 twenty-dollar bills. How many lessons did he take?

   4 lessons

4. **Write About It** Carlos paid a total of $100 to stable his horse. How can finding $100 \div 10$ help you find the number of days Carlos paid for?

   Answers may vary.

Giddy-Up Horse Farm

Riding Lessons: $10 each

Saddle Rental: $5 per hour

Horse Riding: $10 per hour

Stable Fee: $20 per day

Horse Treats: $2 per bag

5. **Write About It** To find the total cost of taking 9 riding lessons, Angie finds $10 \times 9 = 90$. How can she use division to check her result?

   $90 \div 10 = 9$ and
   $90 \div 9 = 10$

Name ______________________ Date ____________

Problem Solving 10.8

Problem-Solving Strategy: Write a Number Sentence

Problem Darius baked 40 treats for the 10 dogs staying at his kennel this week. He gave each dog the same number of treats. How many treats did Darius give each dog?

UNDERSTAND

1. What facts in the problem will you use to help you find what you want to know?

a total of 40 treats; 10 dogs;

Each dog got same number of treats.

PLAN

2. Use the words *separate* and *groups* to describe the problem in your own words.

I need to separate a total of

40 treats into 10 equal groups.

SOLVE

3. Use your chosen operation, the facts given in the problem, and *n* to write a number sentence to model the problem. Then solve the problem.

$40 \div 10 = n$; $n = 4$; Darius

gave 4 treats to each dog.

LOOK BACK

4. What different number sentences can you write to check your solution?

Answers may vary.

Name ______________________ Date ______________

Problem Solving 10.9

Algebra: Division Rules

Solve each problem.

1. Charlie runs a dog-walking service. He has 5 leashes. He uses 1 leash for each dog. How many dogs can Charlie walk at the same time?

   5 dogs

2. Charlie walks the dogs the same distance every day. He walks 7 miles every week. How many miles does he walk each day?

   1 mile

   Show your work.

3. Charlie had 12 dog biscuits. He gave each of the 12 dogs the same number of biscuits. How many biscuits did he give each dog? How do you know?

   1 biscuit, because $12 \div 12 = 1$.

4. **Reasoning** Charlie planned to split his earnings from Friday with his sister if she helped walk the dogs. He did not give any money to his sister. What can you conclude?

   Either his sister did not help walk the dogs on Friday or Charlie did not earn any money on Friday.

5. Write the fact family for 0, 0, and 4. (Remember: you cannot divide by 0.)

   $0 \times 4 = 0$, $4 \times 0 = 0$

   $0 \div 4 = 0$

Name ______________________ Date ____________

Problem Solving 11.1

Divide Using a Multiplication Table

Use the multiplication table at right to solve each problem.

×	0	1	2	3	4	5	6	7	8	9	10
0	0	0	0	0	0	0	0	0	0	0	0
1	0	1	2	3	4	5	6	7	8	9	10
2	0	2	4	6	8	10	12	14	16	18	20
3	0	3	6	9	12	15	18	21	24	27	30
4	0	4	8	12	16	20	24	28	32	36	40
5	0	5	10	15	20	25	30	35	40	45	50
6	0	6	12	18	24	30	36	42	48	54	60
7	0	7	14	21	28	35	42	49	56	63	70
8	0	8	16	24	32	40	48	56	64	72	80
9	0	9	18	27	36	45	54	63	72	81	90
10	0	10	20	30	40	50	60	70	80	90	100

1. What two division sentences describe the shaded row and column in the multiplication table?

   $42 \div 7 = 6$

   $42 \div 6 = 7$

2. **Reasoning** What is the dividend in each of your number sentences for Problem 1? Without looking at the multiplication table, how do you know that this dividend appears somewhere else in the table?

   42; Answers may vary.

3. **What's Wrong?** Nancy says that 0 is written once in every row and column because the quotient of any number divided by 0 is 0. What's wrong?

   You cannot divide by zero.

4. **What If?** Suppose the multiplication table also included 11 and 12 as factors. How many more times would 12 appear as a dividend in the table?

   2 more times

5. **Reasoning** I am a square number dividend. I am an odd number. I appear more than once in the table. What dividend am I?

   9

Name ______________________ Date ____________

Problem Solving 11.2

Algebra: Fact Families

Solve each problem.

1. **Reasoning** If a fact family has only 2 multiplication and division sentences, what do you know about the product and dividend?

   The product and dividend must be a square number.

2. **You Decide** Helen says that she remembers what fact families are by thinking that all the people in her family are related. How do you think this helps her remember?

   Answers will vary.

3. **Reasoning** One dividend in my fact family is 18. One of my divisors is twice one of my quotients. What three numbers are in my fact family? How do you know?

   3, 6, and 18; Explanations may vary.

4. **What's Wrong?** Samuel wrote the fact family below. What did he do wrong?

Samuel
5 x 2 = 10
2 x 5 = 10
2 x 10 = 20
5 x 10 = 50

   Answers may vary.

5. **Represent** Draw an array to show the relationship between the fact family that has the numbers 4, 7, and 28.

   Check students' drawings.

Name ______________________ Date ____________

Divide by 3

Solve each problem.

Show your work.

1. Mr. Gomez planted 24 tulip bulbs in his garden. He planted the same number of tulips in 3 rows. How many tulips did he plant in each row?

   8 tulips

2. In her backyard, Georgia planted 15 sunflowers in 3 pots. She planted the same number of sunflowers in each pot. How many sunflowers are in each pot?

   5 sunflowers

3. **Represent** Robert bought 12 flowers at the Farmers' Market. He wants to put the same number of flowers in each of the vases shown at right. Draw flowers in the vases to show how Robert could fill the vases.

Check students' drawings.

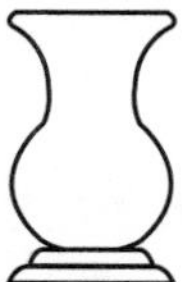

4. **Reasoning** Anne is making 3 bouquets for a wedding. She has 12 gardenias, 30 roses, and 24 lilies. She wants each bouquet to have the same number of each flower. How can she do it?

   4 gardenias, 10 roses, and 8 lilies in each bouquet

5. **Reasoning** Mick spent a total of $15 on roses and irises. The number of irises he bought is one more than the number of roses he bought. Each flower cost $3. How many roses did he buy? How many irises did he buy?

   He bought 3 irises and 2 roses.

Name ______________________ Date ____________

Problem Solving 11.4

Divide by 4

Solve each problem.

1. Mrs. Lewis bought the carton of eggs shown at the right. She wants to use 4 eggs for each omelet. How many omelets can she make?

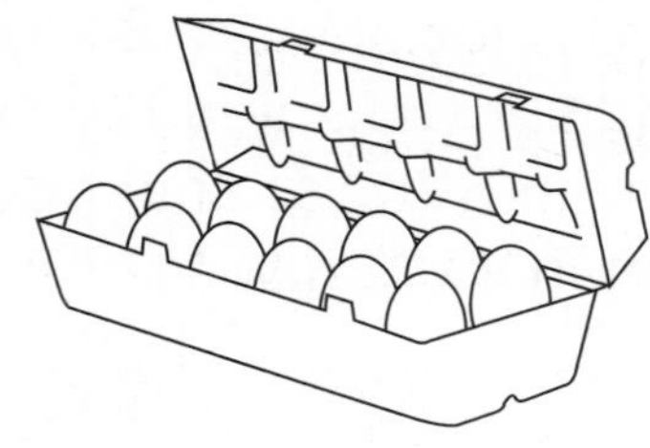

3 omelets

2. Consuela used this recipe to make breakfast trail mix. She filled each bag with 4 cups of the mix. How many bags did she fill?

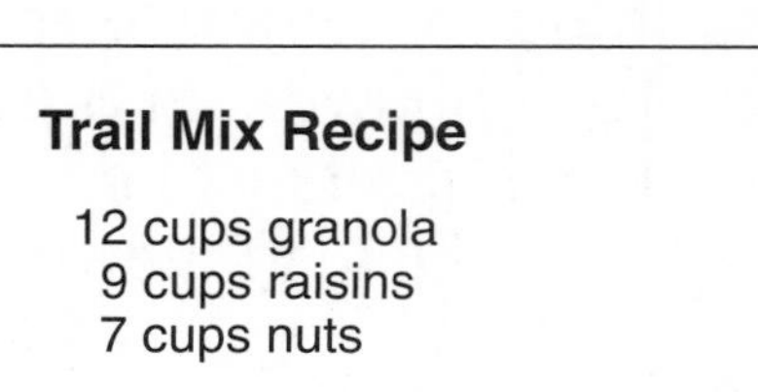

Trail Mix Recipe

12 cups granola
9 cups raisins
7 cups nuts

7 bags

Show your work.

3. There are 4 cups in 1 quart. Alice needs 8 cups of milk to make pancakes for brunch. How many quarts of milk should she buy?

2 quarts

4. **What's Wrong?** Rene bought two dozen muffins. She bought an equal number of blueberry, raisin, wheat, and cranberry muffins. She says that she has 3 of each kind of muffin. What mistake did she make? She did not find correct total number of muffins before dividing. $2 \times 12 = 24$ and $24 \div 4 = 6$. So she has 6 of each kind of muffin.

5. **Reasoning** Alonso made 32 tarts, 24 muffins, and 16 cinnamon buns for his breakfast party. He wants to put the pastries in 4 baskets so that each basket has the same number of each type of pastry. How can he do it?

He can put 8 tarts, 6 muffins, and 4 cinnamon buns in each basket.

Use with text pages 292–294.

Name ______________________ Date ____________

Problem Solving 11.5

Divide by 6

Use Data Mary can fit 6 photographs on each page of her photo albums. The table below shows how many photos she took in each state while visiting the Great Lakes. Use the table to solve each problem.

Great Lake States Photographs	
State	**Number of Photographs**
Illinois	54
Indiana	36
Michigan	42
Minnesota	48
New York	60
Ohio	30
Pennsylvania	18
Wisconsin	24

1. How many pages will Mary fill with the photographs she took in Pennsylvania?

   3 pages

2. Which state's photos will fill exactly 7 album pages?

   Michigan

3. Which state's photos will fill twice as many pages as Ohio's will?

   New York

4. How many states' photographs will fill an odd number of pages?

   4 states

5. **Reasoning** My photos will fill and even number of pages. They will fill fewer pages than Indiana's photos will fill. What state am I?

   Wisconsin

Use with text pages 296–299.

Name ______________________ Date ____________

Problem Solving 11.6

Problem-Solving Strategy: Draw a Picture

Problem Rhonda is building birdhouses for her nephews. For the bird house perch, she cuts a 30-inch dowel into 3 equal pieces. Then she cuts each of those pieces in half. How many pieces of wood did she make for the bird house perches? How long is each piece?

UNDERSTAND

1. What operation will you be modeling? division

PLAN

2. Describe the picture you can draw.

I can draw a line divided into 3 equal pieces and then each of those divided into 2 equal pieces.

SOLVE

3. How many pieces were cut? six

4. How long is each piece? 5 inches

LOOK BACK

5. How can you check your answer?

multiply: 6 pieces × 5 inches = 30 inches

Use with text pages 300–303.

Name ______________________ Date ____________

Divide by 7

For each dance style, the Step-Up Dance School offers the same number of classes each day. Use the table to solve each problem. (1 week = 7 days)

Step-Up Dance School	
Dance Style	**Number of Classes Each Week**
Ballet	70
Salsa	56
Tango	42
Ballroom	63
Tap	28
Flamenco	21
Modern	35
Swing	49

Show your work.

1. How many tap dance classes are taught each day at the school?

   4 classes

2. Brenda wants to take a ballroom dance class on Tuesday. How many classes can she choose from?

   9 classes

3. How many dance styles have an even number of classes each day?

   4 dance styles

4. **What's Wrong?** Flamenco, salsa, and tango are all Spanish dances. Amanda says that Step-Up Dance School offers exactly 21 Spanish dance classes each day. What mistake did Amanda make?

   Answers may vary.

5. **Reasoning** On Friday, Cara took all of the classes offered in two different styles. Oscar took all of the swing classes offered that day. They both took the same number of classes. Which classes did Cara take?

   tap and flamenco

Name ______________________ Date ____________

Problem Solving 11.8

Divide by 8

Use Data Display the data given in the table at left on the pictograph at right. Then use your completed pictograph to solve each problem.

Brain Teaser Web Site Hits	
Day	**Number of Hits**
Monday	72
Tuesday	40
Wednesday	32
Thursday	24
Friday	80

Brain Teaser Web Site Hits	
Monday	
Tuesday	
Wednesday	
Thursday	
Friday	

Each stands for 8 hits.

1. How many pictures did you draw for Monday? Why that many?

   9 pictures; Each picture stands for 8 hits and $72 \div 8 = 9$.

2. **What's Wrong?** Rosa drew 4 pictures for Thursday on her pictograph because $24 \div 6 = 4$. What mistake did Rosa make?

   She thought that each picture stood for 6 hits instead of 8 hits.

3. **Represent** On Saturday, Brain Teaser's Web site got twice as many hits as on Wednesday. How would you show that number of hits on the pictograph? Explain.

   I would draw 8 pictures, $32 + 32 = 64$ and $64 \div 8 = 8$.

4. **What If?** Suppose each on the pictograph stood for 4 hits. How would the number of pictures you drew for each day change?

   Answers may vary.

Name ________________________ Date ____________

Problem Solving 11.9

Divide by 9

Use Data Raul did an inventory of all the books in his collection by subject. He displayed his results in the table below. Use the table to solve each problem.

My Book Collection	
Subject of Book	**Number of Books**
History	72
Art	81
Science	54
Travel	63
Fiction	90
Biography	45
Poetry	27
Cooking	36

Show your work.

1. Raul placed 9 history books on each shelf of one bookcase. How many shelves are in that bookcase?

   8 shelves

2. Raul has 9 empty shelves to hold his cookbooks. If he puts the same number of cookbooks on each shelf, how many will be on each shelf?

   4 cookbooks

3. **Reasoning** Raul wants to fill 9 book shelves with his travel, history, and biography books. He wants each shelf to have the same number of each kind of book. How can he do it?

   He can put 8 history books, 7 travel books, and 5 biography books on each shelf.

4. **What's Wrong?** Raul puts an equal number of each kind of book on 9 shelves. He says that each shelf will have an even number of each kind of book. What's wrong?

   There will be an odd number of art, travel, biography, and poetry books on each shelf.

Name ______________________ Date ____________

Problem Solving 12.1

Hour, Half-Hour, Quarter-Hour

Solve each problem.

1. Jamal's alarm clock went off at quarter after seven. The clock shows what time Jamal actually woke up. Did he wake up when his alarm went off? Explain.

Yes, because the clock shows 7:15.

2. Jamal needs to leave for school at 8:15 A.M. Draw the hour hand and minute hand on the clock to show when Jamal should leave.

Check students' drawings.

3. It takes Jamal a half-hour every morning to get ready for school and a quarter-hour to eat breakfast. How many minutes in all does it take Jamal to get ready for school and eat breakfast each morning?

45 minutes

4. **Reasoning** Jamal takes the city bus to school. Every morning, buses arrive at his stop at 8:45 A.M., 9:00 A.M., and 9:15 A.M. If the pattern continues, what time is the next bus likely to arrive at his stop?

9:30

5. **Estimation** Jamal takes clarinet lessons every Monday at 3:00 P.M. Which time is closer to the start of his lesson, half past three or two forty-five? Explain your answer.

two forty-five, because that is 15 minutes before 3:00 and half past three is 30 minutes after 3:00

Name ______________________ Date ____________

Problem Solving 12.2

Time to Five Minutes

Solve each problem.

1. Maya's flight from Miami was scheduled to take off at 4:35 P.M. The clock shows the time the plane actually took off. Did Maya's flight leave on time? Explain.

No, because the clock shows 4:55, not 4:35.

2. To have enough time to check in, Maya plans to get to the airport at 5 minutes before 2:00. Draw the hour and minute hands on the clock to show that time.

Check students' drawings.

3. The hour hand on Maya's clock points between 3 and 4. The minute hand points to 10. What time does her clock show?

3:50 or 10 minutes before 4

4. **You Decide** A clock shows 10:40. How would you find how many minutes are left in the hour? Explain.

Subtract 40 from 60, because there are 60 minutes in 1 hour.

5. **What's Wrong?** Maya's plane arrives at 7:20 P.M. She tells her sister to pick her up at the airport at 40 minutes before 7. What should Maya have told her sister?

Maya should have told her sister to pick her up at 40 minutes before 8, or 20 minutes after 7.

Name ______________________ Date ____________

Problem Solving 12.3

Time to the Minute

Use Data The table below shows the time each student started to read his or her book report. Use the table to solve each problem.

Book Report Times	
Student	**Starting Time**
Brent	2:37 P.M.
Chad	3:28 P.M.
Kate	2:06 P.M.
Luis	3:48 P.M.
Manuel	2:59 P.M.
Naomi	3:47 P.M.
Tameeka	3:24 P.M.
Will	2:15 P.M.

1. Which student started reading at 28 minutes after 3?

   Chad

2. Which students started to read their reports between 2:30 P.M. and 3:00 P.M.?

   Brent and Manuel

3. Using words, write the starting time for the student who started reading his or her report first.

   six minutes after two P.M.

4. **Estimation** Who started to read closest to 3:00 P.M.? Who started closest to 4:00 P.M.?

   Manuel started closest to 3:00 P.M. Luis started closest to 4:00 P.M.

5. **Represent** Draw hands on the clock below to show the time the last student started reading.

Check students' drawings.

Use with text pages 334–335.

Name ______________________ Date __________

Elapsed Time

Solve each problem.

1. Miguel promised to practice the piano for 45 minutes. The clocks at right show what time he started and stopped practicing. Did Miguel keep his promise? Explain.

Yes, from 2:10 to 2:55 is 45 minutes.

2. Miguel practiced 3 songs between 10:00 A.M. and 10:45 A.M. He spent the same amount of time on each song. At what time did he start practicing each song?

10:00 A.M., 10:15 A.M., and 10:30 A.M.

3. Miguel's piano lesson started at 5:00 P.M. First, he reviewed scales for 15 minutes. Then he played the songs he learned last week for 25 minutes. The last half-hour of his lesson was spent learning new songs. At what time did his lesson end?

6:10 P.M.

4. **Reasoning** Miguel rented studio time to record his piano playing. Each hour at the studio costs $50. He started recording at noon. If he pays a total of $200 for his studio time, at what time did he stop recording?

4:00 P.M.

Name ______________________ Date ______________

Problem Solving 12.5

Use a Calendar

Use the calendar at right to solve Problems 1–5.

1. **Estimation** About how many weeks are there between the new moon in February and the full moon in February?

   about 2 weeks

2. How many days before Presidents' Day is Valentine's Day?

   4 days

3. In a leap year, February has one more day than the calendar shown at right. What date comes after February 28 in a leap year? What date comes after February 28 in all other years?

   February 29; March 1

4. **Reasoning** Kendra's birthday is in February. The date is a two-digit odd number less than 29. The sum of the digits is a two-digit number. What is Kendra's birthday?

   February 19

5. Read the calendar poem at right. How many months have 31 days? How do you know from reading the poem?

   7 months; *Explanations may vary.*

February						
Sun	Mon	Tue	Wed	Thu	Fri	Sat
					1	2 Groundhog Day
3	4	5	6	7	8 New Moon/ Chinese New Year	9
10	11	12	13	14 Valentine's Day	15	16
17	18 Presidents' Day	19	20	21	22	23 Full Moon
24	25	26	27	28		

Thirty days have September
April, June, and November.
All the rest have thirty-one
Except February, she alone
Has eight days and a score*
Til leap year gives her one more.
* A score is 20.

Name ______________________ Date ____________

Problem Solving 12.6

Problem-Solving Application: Use a Schedule

Problem Andrea needs to get to New York by noon. She cannot leave before 9:00 A.M. Which train should she take?

Train Schedule to New York		
Train	**Depart**	**Arrive**
Daily	7:30 A.M.	10:40 A.M.
Metroliner	8:35 A.M.	11:43 A.M.
Express	10:20 A.M.	11:35 A.M.
Tourliner	10:45 A.M.	12:17 P.M.

UNDERSTAND

1. What information does the schedule give you? departure and arrival times for 4 trains to New York

PLAN

2. What will you look for in the column of the schedule labeled *Depart*? What will you look for in the column of the schedule labeled *Arrive*?

times after 9:00 A.M.;

times before 12:00 P.M.

SOLVE

3. Which train leaves after 9:00 A.M. AND arrives before noon?

the Express

LOOK BACK

4. The Tourliner also leaves after 9:00 A.M. Why can't Andrea take that train? She needs to arrive before noon, and the Tourliner arrives after noon.

Name ______________________ Date ____________

Temperature: Degrees Fahrenheit and Celsius

Solve each problem.

1. **Reasoning** Jack went water skiing today. Was the temperature outside 30˚F or 30˚C? Explain.

   30°C; 30°F would be too cold to go water skiing.

2. Water freezes at 0˚C and 32˚F. The temperature is 5˚, and the water in a pail is frozen. Is it 5 degrees Celsius or 5 degrees Fahrenheit?

   degrees Fahrenheit

3. The thermometers below show the temperatures when school started and ended. How many degrees did the temperature rise?

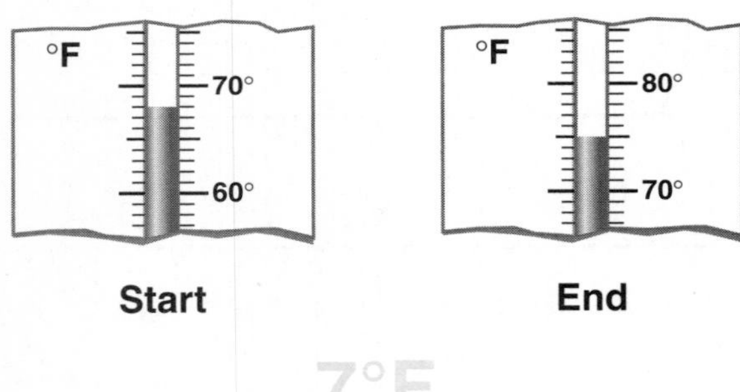

   7°F

4. **Predict** The temperature at the bottom of a mountain is 50˚F. In general, temperatures drop 3˚F every 1,000 feet higher up the mountain you go. The mountain is 3,000 feet tall. What is the temperature likely to be at the top of the mountain?

   41°F

Name ______________________ Date ____________

Measure to the Nearest Inch

For Problems 1–3, estimate and then measure each of Keith's school supply objects to the nearest inch. Then use your measurements to solve Problems 4–5.

1. 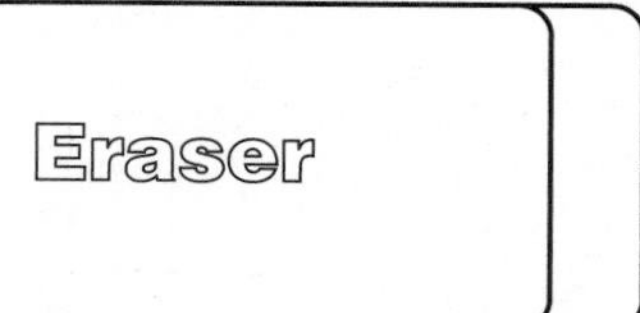

Estimates may vary

2 in.

2. 

2 in.

3. 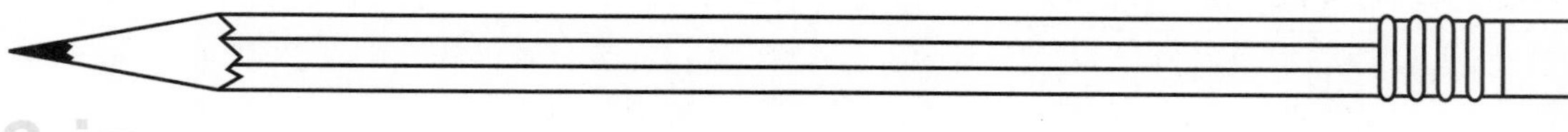

6 in.

4. **Reasoning** There are 12 inches in 1 foot. Which of the school supply items is closest to $\frac{1}{2}$ foot long?

   the pencil

5. **Estimation** About how many times longer is the pencil than the pencil sharpener?

   about 3 times longer

Name ______________________ Date ____________

Problem Solving 13.2

Measure to the Nearest Half Inch

Measure each ribbon to the nearest half inch. Then use your measurements to solve Problems 5–7.

1. $2\frac{1}{2}$ in.

2. 2 in.

3. 4 in.

4. $6\frac{1}{2}$ in.

5. List the ribbons above in order from shortest to longest. Use the pictures on each ribbon to name it.

heart, star, diamond, triangle

6. How many half inches are there in one whole inch? How many half inches long is the heart ribbon?

2 half inches; 4 half inches

7. **Reasoning** To the nearest half inch, two ribbons combined have the same length as another ribbon. What are the two combined ribbons? What is the other ribbon?

The star and diamond ribbons combined are the same length as the triangle ribbon.

Name ______________________ Date ____________

Problem Solving 13.3

Customary Units of Length

Use the table to solve Problems 1–5.

Professional Football Measurements	
Height of Goal Post Crossbar	10 feet
Length of Ball	11 inches
Length of End Zone	10 yards
Length of Field	100 yards
Width of Field	160 feet
Width of Goal Post Crossbar	$18\frac{1}{2}$ feet

Show your work.

1. How many feet long is each end zone? What is the combined length, in feet, of the field's two end zones?

   30 feet; 60 feet

2. Give the width of the goal post crossbar using only yards and inches.

   6 yards, 6 inches

3. How many times longer is the field than the end zone?

   10 times longer

4. **You Decide** Is the football field 3 feet long, 30 feet long, or 300 feet long? Explain your choice.

   300 feet long; There are 3 feet in 1 yard, and the field is 100 yards long: 100 + 100 + 100 = 300.

5. **What's Wrong?** Tyler says that the football field is wider than it is long. What mistake did he make?

   He did not pay attention to the units. 160 feet < 100 yards.

Name ______________________ Date ____________

Problem-Solving Strategy: Use Logical Reasoning

Problem Jeremy, Erin, Mel, and Paco competed in the long jump. Their jump lengths were 9 feet, 10 feet, 11 feet, and 12 feet. Paco jumped the farthest. Erin jumped an even number of feet. Mel jumped farther than Jeremy. How far did they each jump?

1. What were the four jump lengths?

9 feet, 10 feet, 11 feet, and 12 feet

PLAN

2. How can you use a table and logical reasoning to organize the facts? Make a table with two columns, one for the four students' names and one for their jump lengths. Then use the facts to fill in the table.

SOLVE

3. How far did they each jump?

Paco jumped 12 feet, Erin jumped 10 feet, Mel jumped 11 feet, and Jeremy jumped 9 feet.

4. Do your answers match all of the facts given in the problem? Explain. Yes; 12 is greater than 9, 10, or 11; 10 is an even number; and 11 > 9.

Name ______________________ Date ______________

Estimate and Measure Capacity

For Problems 1–4, use the labeled capacity in each pair of containers to estimate the capacity of the unlabeled container in the pair. Then solve problems 5–8.

1. About how many cups of hot chocolate will fill the large mug?

about 2 cups

2. About how many pints of yogurt are in the small carton?

4 pints

about 2 pints

3. About many quarts of milk are in the small jug?

about 4 quarts

4. About how many gallons of water will fill the large cooler bottle?

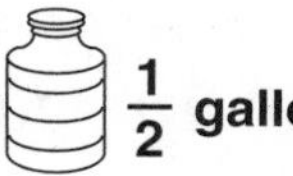

about 1 gallon

5. Which container above has a capacity of 1 pint?

the large mug

6. Which container above has a capacity of 1 quart?

the small yogurt container

7. Which containers above have a capacity of 1 gallon?

the small milk jug and the large cooler bottle

8. Which container above has the greatest capacity? Which container above has the least capacity?

The large milk jug; the small mug

Name ______________________ Date ______________

Problem Solving 13.6

Customary Units of Capacity

Jennifer used the recipes below to make drinks for her party. Use the recipes to solve each problem.

Berry Shake

Mix in a blender:
2 cups plain yogurt
2 teaspoons vanilla extract
3 cups frozen raspberries, thawed
1 pint strawberry ice cream

Fruit Punch

Mix in large punchbowl:
1 gallon orange juice
2 quarts pineapple juice
6 pints lime sherbet
1 quart ginger ale

Show your work.

1. How many pints of plain yogurt did Jennifer use for the berry shake?

   1 pint

2. How many cups of ginger ale did Jennifer use for the fruit punch?

   4 cups

3. Did Jennifer use more pineapple juice or lime sherbet in the punch? How many pints more?

   lime sherbet; 2 pints more

4. Jennifer used the same amount of 2 ingredients to make the shakes. Which ingredients are they?

   plain yogurt and strawberry ice cream

5. **Reasoning** The difference between these two punch ingredient amounts is 6 pints. What are the ingredients?

   orange juice and ginger ale

Use with text pages 370–371.

Name ______________________ Date ____________

Customary Units of Weight

Use Data The table below shows the normal weight of balls used in some professional sports. Use the table to solve each problem.

Professional Sports Balls	
Sport	**Ball Weight**
Baseball	5 ounces
Basketball	22 ounces
Bowling	16 pounds
Cricket	6 ounces
Golf	1 ounce
Rugby	15 ounces
Tennis	2 ounces
Volleyball	10 ounces

Show your work.

1. Which ball is the heaviest? Which ball is lightest?

   bowling ball; golf ball

2. Which balls weigh more than 1 pound?

   basketball and bowling ball

3. Which sports' balls weigh less than $\frac{1}{2}$ pound?

   baseball, cricket, golf, and tennis

4. **Reasoning** You place a rugby ball on one pan of a balance scale. How many baseballs should you place on the other pan to balance the scale?

   3 baseballs

5. List all the pairs of balls for which the combined weight of the two balls is 1 pound.

   cricket ball and volleyball; golf ball and rugby ball

Name ______________________ Date ______________

Problem Solving 13.8

Problem-Solving Decision: Too Much or Too Little Information

Problem Apples at the Farmers' Market are sold by the bushel and by the pound. One bushel of apples weighs 42 pounds. Apples cost $1 per pound. A bushel of apples costs $25. Tony bought 3 bushels of apples. How much did they weigh in all?

1. What do you want to know?

the total weight of the apples Tony bought

PLAN

2. What facts are needed to solve the problem?

Each bushel weighs 42 pounds.
Tony bought 3 bushels.

SOLVE

3. Choose one operation and use it to solve the problem.

$42 + 42 + 42 = 126$ or $42 \times 3 = 126$
Tony bought 126 pounds of apples.

4. How could you check your answer?

Answers will vary.

Use with text page 376.

Name ______________________ Date ____________

Problem Solving 14.1

Centimeter and Millimeter

For Problems 1–2, estimate the length of each tropical fish. Then measure each to the nearest centimeter. Use your measurements to solve Problems 3–5.

1. Coolie Loach

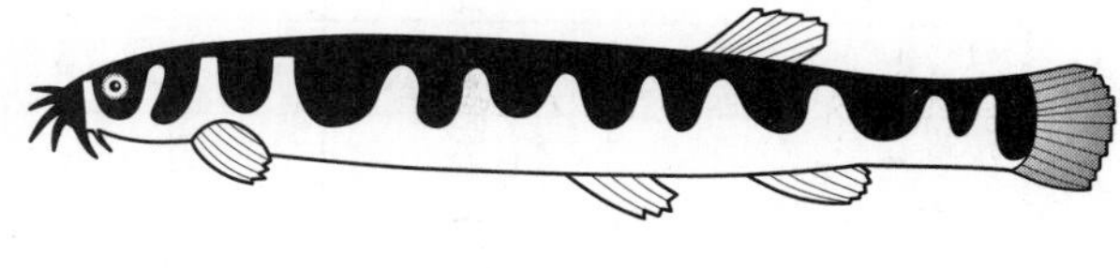

8 centimeters

2. Bloodfin

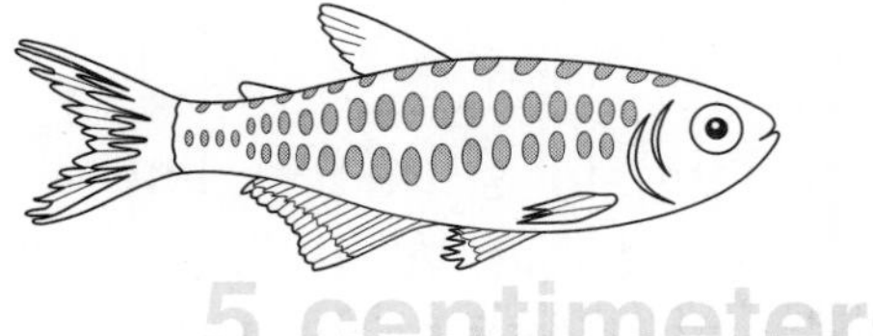

5 centimeters

3. Which fish above is closest to 1 decimeter long? Which fish is closest to one-half decimeter long?

Coolie loach; bloodfin

4. A blue gularis is twice as long as a bloodfin. How long is the blue gularis?

10 cm or 1 dm

5. **You Decide** A clown loach in a fish tank is 10 centimeters long. In the wild, a clown loach grows 3 times longer. Phil says a wild clown loach is 30 centimeters long. Wendy says it is 3 decimeters long. Who is right? Explain.

They are both right, because 3×10 cm = 30 cm, and 30 cm = 3 dm.

Estimates of lengths will vary. Students should use their finger widths to estimate.

Name ______________________ Date ____________

Problem Solving 14.2

Meter and Kilometer

Use Problems 1–3 to complete the table below. Then use your table to solve each problem.

1. The baird's whale is the shortest whale listed in the table. Write "baird's whale" in the correct row of the table.

2. The blue whale is the longest whale listed in the table. Write "blue whale" in the correct row of the table.

3. **Reasoning** The humpback whale is longer than the gray whale, but shorter than the sperm whale. Write each of these 3 whale names in their correct rows to finish the table.

Whale Lengths	
Whale	**Length**
humpback whale	15 m
baird's whale	10 m
gray whale	14 m
blue whale	32 m
sperm whale	18 m

4. **What's Wrong?** Joey says that 3 blue whales end-to-end are about 1 kilometer long. What's wrong with Joey's statement?

1 kilometer = 1,000 meters, and 3 blue whales end-to-end would be only about 100 meters.

5. Sperm whales are the deepest divers of all whales. They dive 3 kilometers in search of giant squid to eat. How many meters do sperm whales dive?

3,000 meters

Name ______________________ Date ____________

Problem Solving 14.3

Metric Units of Capacity

For a science experiment, the third-graders used the recipes below to make samples of ocean saltwater. Use the recipes to solve each problem.

Recipe for Bucket of Ocean

Mix in a large bucket:

19 L tap water
400 mL table salt
3 mL baking soda
11 mL dietary salt substitute
120 mL epsom salt

Recipe for Bathtub of Ocean

Mix in a bathtub:

150 L tap water
3 L table salt
25 mL baking soda
80 mL dietary salt substitute
960 mL epsom salt

1. How many milliliters of tap water are used for the bucket of ocean?

   19,000 mL

2. How many milliliters of table salt are used for the bathtub of ocean?

   3,000 mL

3. Which recipe has an ingredient whose amount is closest to 1 liter? What ingredient is it? bathtub of ocean; epsom salt

4. **Reasoning** The third-graders used a kitchen measuring cup to measure their ingredients. Each cup holds one-half liter. For which ingredients in either recipe did they have to fill the measuring cup more than once?

   ____

5. **What's Wrong?** Andrea says that the same amount of baking soda is used in the bucket of ocean as the amount of table salt used in the bathtub of ocean. What mistake did Andrea make? She did not pay attention to the units.

4. tap water in both recipes, and table salt and epsom salt in the bathtub recipe

Name ______________________ Date ____________

Problem Solving 14.4

Problem-Solving Strategy: Work Backward

Problem Judy found an old plank on the beach. She cut off 12 centimeters where the plank was broken. Then she cut the remaining plank into 3 equal pieces. Each piece is now 20 centimeters long. How long was the plank she found on the beach?

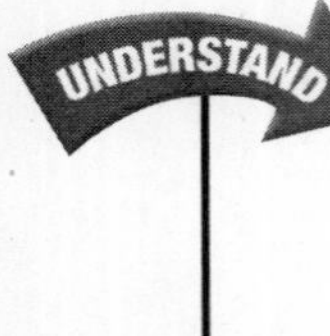

1. What do you want to know?

____

PLAN

2. With what amount will you start working backward?

____

3. Write the solution to the problem in a complete sentence.

____

4. How can you work forward to check that your answer is reasonable?

____

Name ______________________ Date ____________

Problem Solving 14.5

Metric Units of Mass

River dolphins live in muddy rivers of South America and Asia. Most are much smaller than their more familiar cousins, the ocean dolphins.

Use Data Use the table to solve each problem.

River Dolphins		
Dolphin	**Calf Mass**	**Adult Mass**
Amazon	7 kg	120 kg
Chinese	4,000 g	130 kg
Franciscana	8 kg	40 kg
Ganges	7,500 g	80 kg

1. Which calf has the greater mass, an Amazon river dolphin or a Ganges river dolphin?

   Ganges river dolphin

2. Which adult river dolphin has twice the mass of an adult Franciscana river dolphin?

   Ganges river dolphin

3. Which river dolphin calf has twice the mass of a Chinese river dolphin?

   Franciscana river dolphin

4. For which two dolphin calves is the difference in their masses three kg?

   Amazon river dolphin and Chinese river dolphin

5. **What If?** Suppose all the calf masses were written in grams. Which river dolphin would have the greatest mass? Which would have the least mass?

   Greatest: Franciscana river dolphin; Least: Chinese river dolphin

Name ______________________ Date ____________

Problem Solving 15.1

Lines, Line Segments, Rays, and Angles

Solve each problem. Sample answers given.

1. **Write About It** Use geometric terms to describe this compass rose.

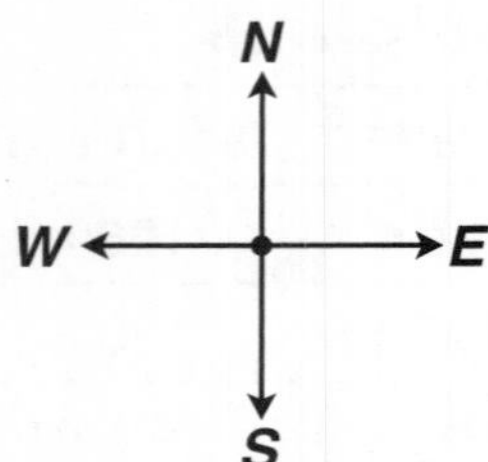

The compass is formed by 2 perpendicular lines.

2. **Write About It** Use geometric terms to describe the hands on this clock.

The two hands together form a right angle.

3. **Reasoning** Two angles combined form a right angle. What must be true about each of those two angles? How do you know?

They both must be acute angles. The sum of the two angles is 90°, so each angle must be less than 90°.

4. **Represent** Main Street runs straight east across town. Oak Street runs straight west across town. Draw these streets. How can you describe these two streets as lines? Explain your thinking.

They are parallel lines. A street running east will never intersect a street running west.

Name ______________________ Date ____________

Problem Solving 15.2

Classify Plane Figures

Solve each problem.

1. How many polygons are shown in the figure below? Name them all.

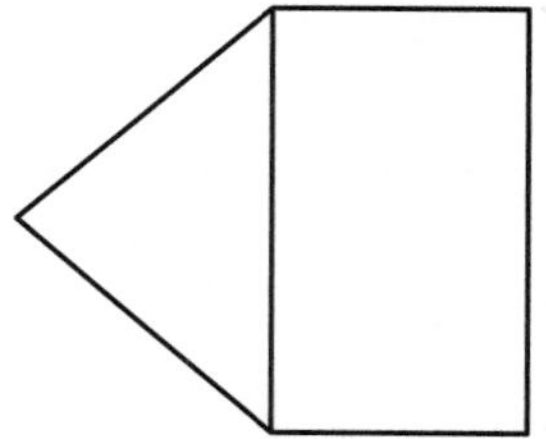

1 rectangle; 1 triangle; 1 pentagon

2. **Represent.** Draw one triangle on the picture in Problem 1 to change it to a hexagon.

Check students' drawings.

3. **Reasoning** I am a polygon. I have one more vertex than a rectangle has. What am I?

a pentagon

4. **Reasoning** I am a polygon. I have twice as many sides as another polygon. I have less than 8 sides. What am I?

a hexagon

5. **What's Wrong?** Jamal says that a circle is a polygon because it is a flat plane figure that is closed. What's wrong?

A circle is not a polygon, because it is not made with line segments.

Name ______________________ Date ____________

Problem Solving 15.3

Classify Triangles

Solve each problem.

1. How many triangles are shown in the figure below? Label each triangle with its special name.

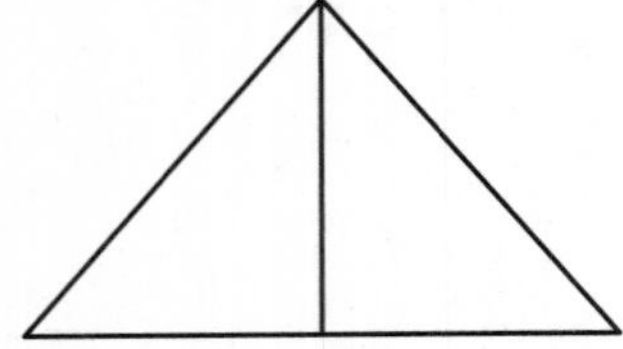

3 triangles; *Check labels.*

2. **Reasoning** How are a square and an equilateral triangle alike? How are they different?

They have equal sides; They are different because they have different numbers of sides.

3. **Write About It** How is classifying a triangle as a right triangle different from classifying it as equilateral, scalene, or isosceles?

When you classify a triangle as a right triangle, you are classifying it by its angles. When you classify it as an equilateral, scalene, or isosceles, you are classifying it by its sides.

4. **Reasoning** The triangle shown below is an isosceles triangle. What is the length of its unlabeled side? Explain how you know.

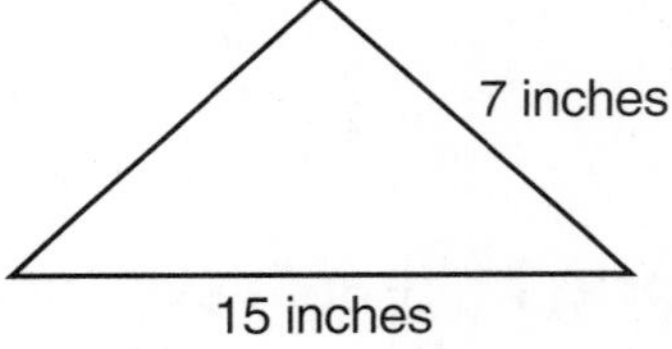

7 inches; two of its sides are the same length, and the unlabeled side is shorter than the side labeled 15 feet.

Name ______________________ Date ____________

Problem Solving 15.4

Classify Quadrilaterals

Solve each problem.

1. How many quadrilaterals are part of the figure shown below? If any has a special name, name it.

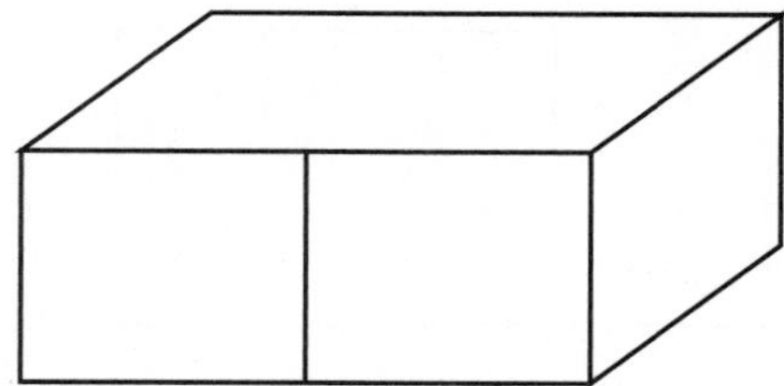

5 quadrilaterals:
3 rectangles;
2 parallelograms

2. When you draw one diagonal across a rectangle, what two polygons are formed?

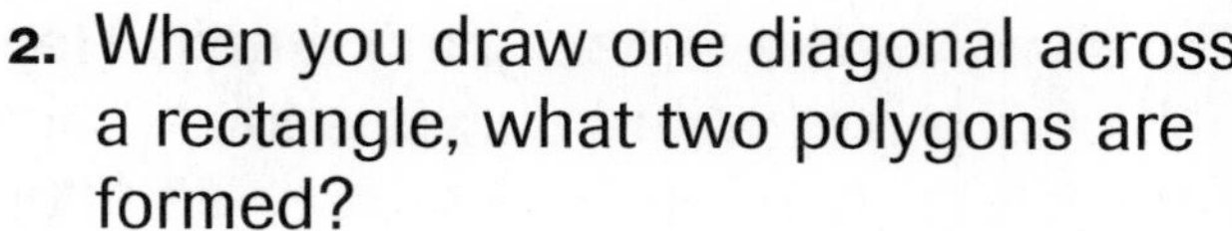

2 right triangles

3. **Reasoning** I am a polygon with 4 right angles. I am not a square.

a rectangle

4. **Represent** How many diagonals can be drawn for any quadrilateral? Draw a picture in the space below to explain your answer.

2 diagonals; check students' drawings.

5. **You Decide** Jay says that this polygon is a rectangle. Paul says that it is a parallelogram. Who is right? Explain your choice.

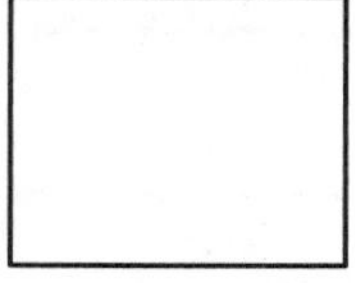

They are both right. It is a rectangle because it has 4 sides and 4 right angles, and all rectangles are parallelograms.

Name ______________________ Date ______________

Problem Solving 15.5

Problem-Solving Strategy: Find a Pattern

Problem Becky is designing a quilt. Her design for the first half of one row of the quilt is shown below. If she continues her pattern, what are the next three figures likely to be?

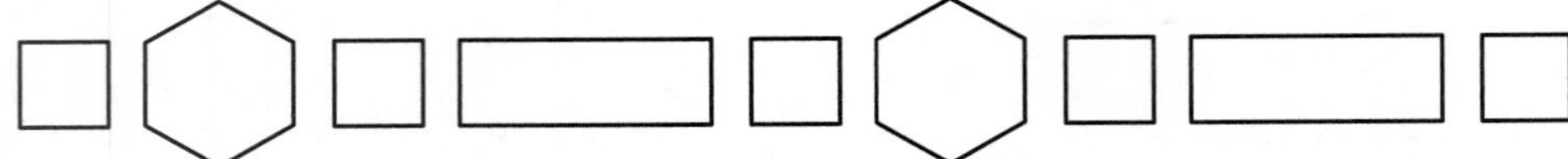

UNDERSTAND

1. What do you want to know?

   the next three figures in the pattern

PLAN

2. Once you find the pattern, what do you need to do to solve the problem?

   extend the pattern

SOLVE

3. What is the last figure shown in the pattern? What three figures always follow that figure in the pattern? a square; hexagon, square, and rectangle

LOOK BACK

4. Give each figure in the pattern a different number. Use the numbers to model the pattern. How can this help you check that your solution is reasonable?

   Numbers students use will vary.

   I can find a pattern in the numbers and extend it to the next three numbers.

Name ______________________ Date ______________

Solid Figures

Use the objects shown below to solve Problems 1–4.

Paperweight	Tissue Box	Soup Can	Globe	Pin Box	Party Hat

1. **Reasoning** Which objects will NOT roll smoothly?

paperweight, tissue box, and pin box

2. **You Decide** Chantall says that the pin box is a cube. Emily say that it is a rectangular prism. Who is right? Explain your choice.

They are both right; the pin box is a cube, and a cube is a kind of rectangular prism.

3. **Write About It** Sort all the objects into two groups. Explain your groupings.

Answers may vary.

4. **Reasoning** The picture below shows an unfolded cardboard container. The dotted lines show where to fold. When the container is folded, what solid figure will its shape be?

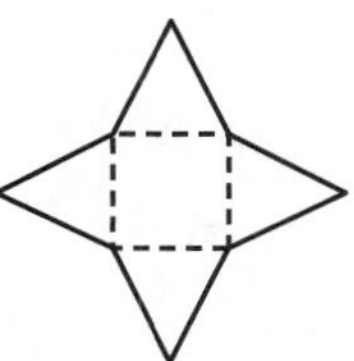

a pyramid

Name ______________________ Date ______________

Explore Solid Figures

Linda painted one face of each of her wooden solid figures. Then she pressed the painted face onto paper, using it like a stamp. For Problems 1–4, use the given figures that Linda stamped onto paper to solve each problem.

1. What solid figure did Linda use to stamp this shape? How do you know?

   A pyramid; only pyramids have triangular faces.

2. **Reasoning** Can you tell what solid figure Linda used to stamp this shape? Explain.

   No; it could be the bottom of a cone, or either flat face of a cylinder.

3. **Reasoning** Linda wants to paint each face of a square pyramid a different color. How many colors will she use?

   5 colors

4. **Reasoning** I am a solid figure with 6 faces, 8 vertices, and 12 edges. My edges are NOT all the same length. What am I?

   a rectangular prism

Use with text pages 434–436.

Name ______________________ Date ____________

Problem Solving 16.1

Congruent Figures

Solve each problem.

1. Paco drew a square with sides that are each 15 inches long. Ellen drew a figure congruent to Paco's square. What figure did Ellen draw? What is the length of each of its sides?

   a square; 15 inches

2. Susan drew an equilateral triangle. One of its sides is 9 centimeters long. Jason drew a triangle congruent to Susan's triangle. How long were the sides of Jason's triangle?

   9 centimeters

3. **Write About It** Explain how you would draw a line segment congruent to the one shown below.

   Answers may vary.

4. **Reasoning** Kelly drew a rectangle. Aaron drew a square congruent to Kelly's rectangle. How is this possible?

   The rectangle that Kelly drew was a square.

5. **What's Wrong?** Ruth drew a hexagon with 2-inch sides. Phil drew a five-sided polygon with 2-inch sides. Phil says his figure is congruent to Ruth's. What's wrong?

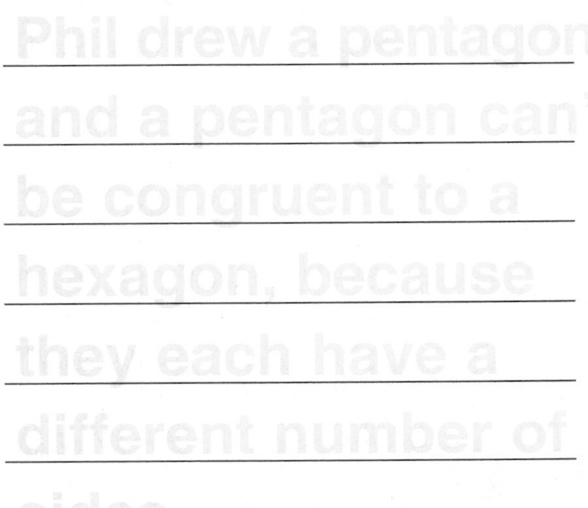

   Phil drew a pentagon, and a pentagon can't be congruent to a hexagon, because they each have a different number of sides.

6. **Represent** Use this grid paper to draw a figure that is congruent to the figure shown.

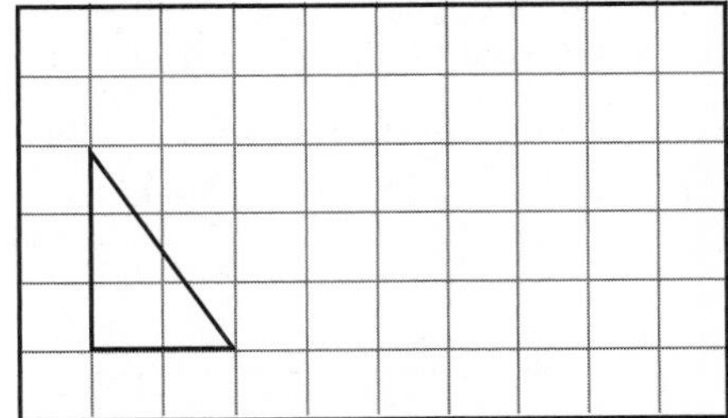

   Check students' drawings

Use with text pages 442–443.

Name ____________________ Date __________

Problem Solving 16.2

Similar Figures

Solve each problem.

1. Look at the drawings of the bicycle and tricycle at right. Which has similar wheels? Which has congruent wheels?

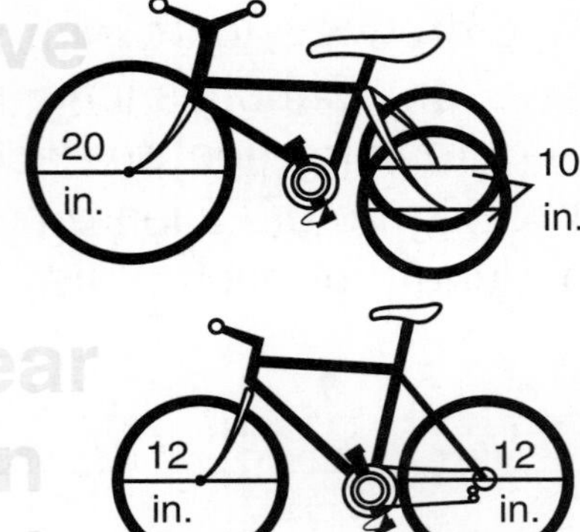

Both have similar wheels. The wheels on the bicycle are congruent. The rear wheels on the tricycle are congruent.

2. **Predict** Mandy is making this pattern with similar figures. What will the next figure in her pattern most likely be? What will be its side lengths?

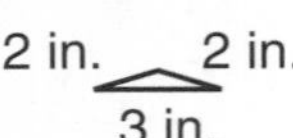

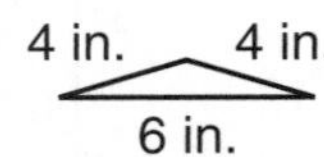

8 in. 8 in. 12 in.

an isosceles triangle with sides of 16 in., 16 in., 24 in.

3. **What's Wrong?** Abby says that these two triangles are not similar because their sides have different lengths. What's wrong?

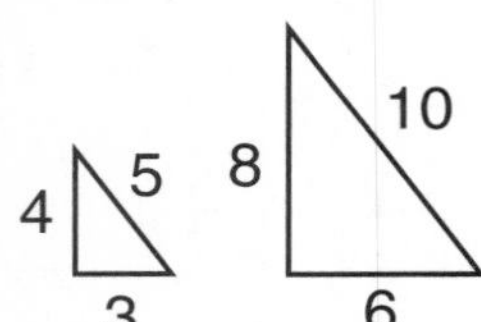

Answers may vary.

4. **You Decide** Matt says that all squares are similar. Anita says that all rectangles are similar. Who is right? Explain your choice.

Matt is right, because all squares have the same shape. Rectangles can have many different shapes.

Name ______________________ Date ____________

Line of Symmetry

Solve each problem.

1. A standard deck of playing cards has 4 suits—clubs, diamonds, hearts, and spades. Which suit picture has the most lines of symmetry? How many?

diamond; 2 lines

2. Ariana's school locker number is shown at right. Which digit has two lines of symmetry? Which digit has only one line of symmetry? Which digit has no lines of symmetry?

3 5 8

8; 3; 5

3. **You Decide** Which of these triangles does NOT have at least one line of symmetry?

the scalene triangle

4. **You Decide** Which quadrilateral has more lines of symmetry, the square or the rectangle?

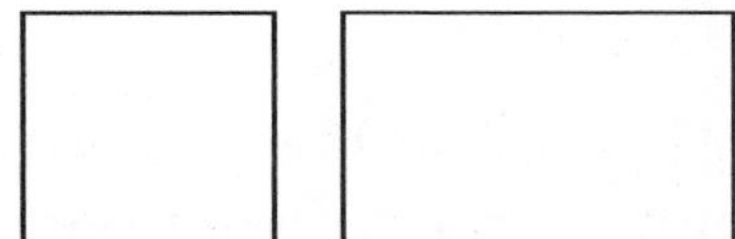

the square

5. **Write About It** Explain how you can check to see whether the line drawn is a line of symmetry for this figure.

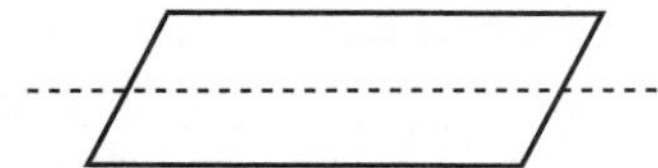

Answers may vary.

Name ______________________ Date ____________

Problem Solving 16.4

Transformations

For Problems 1–4, tell how you would move the last figure to complete the pattern. Write *slide, flip,* or *turn.*

1.  SSƧSSƧS

slide

2.  L L < < L L < < L

slide

3.

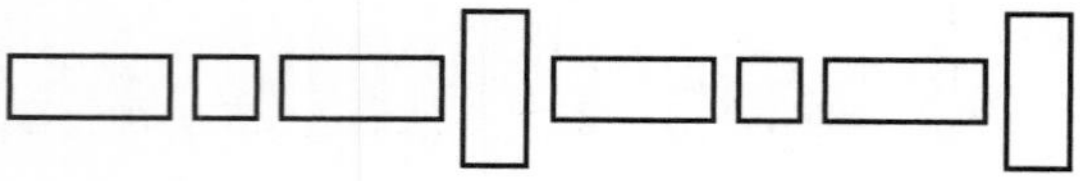

turn

4.

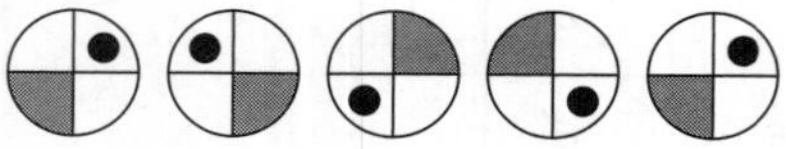

flip or turn

5. **Predict** Look at the pattern below. In what position will the tenth arrow be? How do you know?

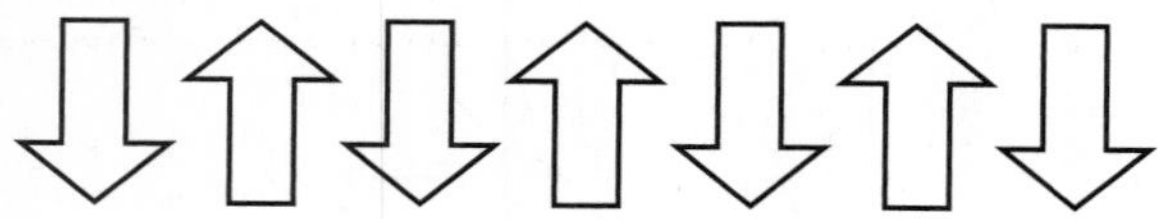

pointing up; the eighth arrow points up, the ninth arrow points down, and the tenth arrow points up.

Name ______________________ Date ____________

Problem-Solving Application: Visual Thinking

Problem Randy folded each of the boxes shown below and placed a candle in each. Two of the candles he boxed are shown at right. What was the shape of the third candle that Randy boxed?

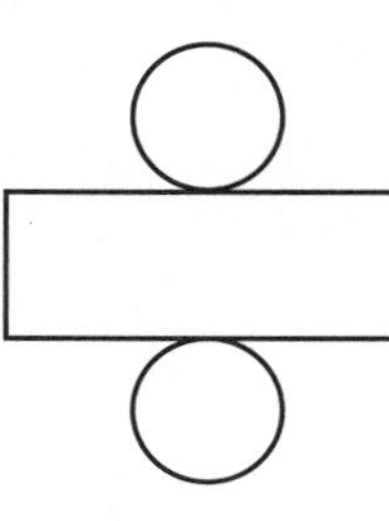

Box A

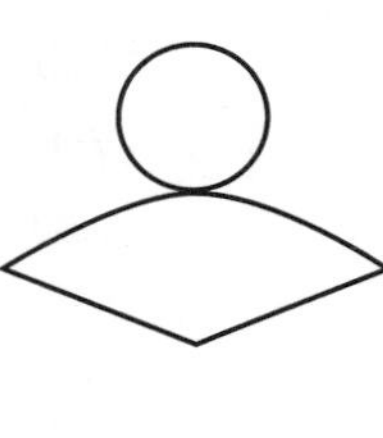

Box B

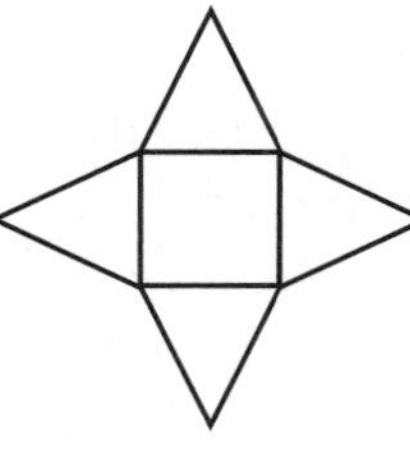

Box C

UNDERSTAND

1. What do you want to know?

the shape of the third candle not shown

PLAN

2. What will you visualize for each box?

its shape when folded

SOLVE

3. What is the shape of the box not used for the white or gray candle?

a cone

LOOK BACK

4. What is the shape of the white candle? Which box has that shape?

a cylinder; Box A

Name ______________________ Date ______________

Problem Solving 17.1

Explore Perimeter

Solve each problem. **Show your work.**

1. Yolanda wants to buy a frame for her school photo. To estimate its perimeter, she uses 24 toothpicks to surround the photo. Each toothpick is about 2 inches long. About how many inches long is the perimeter of Yolanda's school photo?

   48 inches

2. **Predict** An art supply store sells photograph frames in 5 sizes. The perimeters of the first three frames are 20 inches, 24 inches, and 28 inches. If this pattern continues, what are the perimeters of the next two frames likely to be?

   32 inches and 36 inches

3. **You Decide** Connie is making a wooden frame for a painting. Should she estimate its perimeter with paper clips or measure its perimeter with a ruler? Explain your choice.

   Answers and explanations may vary.

4. Jamie wants to make a frame for a postcard. To measure its perimeter, he wraps a string around the edges of the postcard. What should he do next to find the perimeter of the postcard in inches?

   Measure the length of the string with an inch ruler.

5. **Reasoning** Frank has two mirrors to frame. One mirror is a square and the other mirror is an octagon. Each side of both mirrors is 5 inches long. Which mirror's frame will need more wood?

   the octagon

Use with text pages 462–463.

Name ______________________ Date ____________

Problem Solving 17.2

Find Perimeter

The diagram below shows Julie's plan for her garden. Use the diagram to solve Problems 1–4.

Show your work.

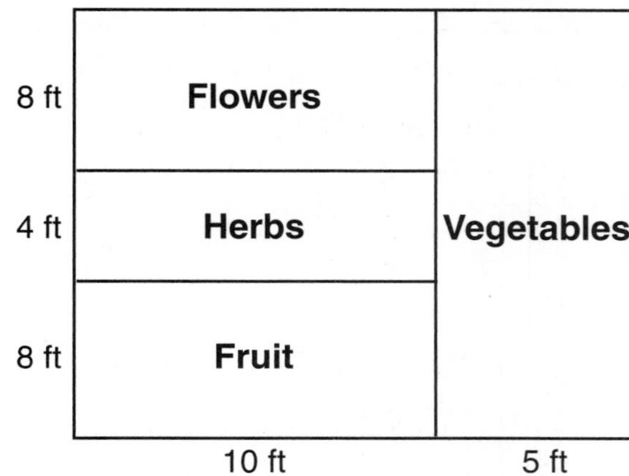

1. What is the perimeter of the herb section of Julie's garden?

   28 feet

2. What did Julie plant in the largest section in her garden? What is the perimeter of that section?

   vegetables; 50 ft

3. Which two sections of her garden have the same perimeter? What is their perimeter?

   flowers and fruit; 36 ft

4. **Multistep** If each foot of fencing costs $3, how much will it cost to fence the outside of the garden?

   $210

5. **Reasoning** Julie plans to build a fish pond near her garden. The pond will be in the shape of an equilateral triangle. Its perimeter will be 12 feet. What will be the length of each side of the fish pond?

   4 feet

Use with text pages 464–466.

Name ____________________ Date ____________

Problem Solving 17.3

Explore Area

Estimate the area of each merit patch that Phil earned at camp. Each □ = 1 square unit.

1. **Hiking**

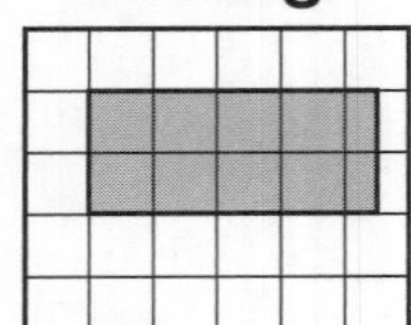

9 square units

Canoeing

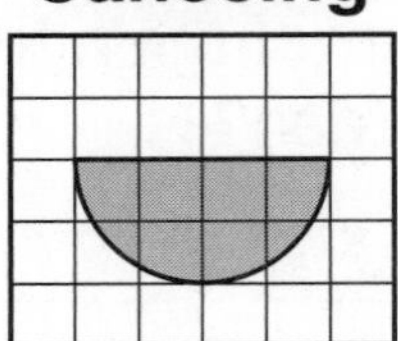

7 square units

Rock Climbing

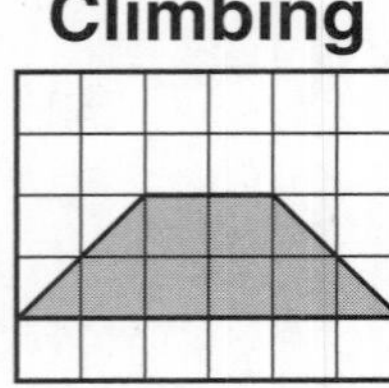

8 square units

Fishing

12 square units

2. Phil plans to sew all his merit patches on his camp jacket. Which patch will cover the largest space on his jacket?

fishing

3. Which of Phil's patches are quadrilaterals? Which of those patches will cover more of Phil's jacket? How much more?

Hiking and climbing; hiking; 1 square unit more

4. **What If?** Suppose Phil earns two canoeing patches. If he sews them next to each other, what shape can they form? About how many square units of his jacket will that shape cover?

A circle, about 14 square units

5. **Represent** To see what the camp mountain climbing patch looks like, draw two line segments on the rock climbing patch to change it to a triangle. Then estimate the area of the mountain climbing patch.

Check students' drawings; 9 square units

Name ______________________ Date ____________

Problem Solving 17.4

Find Area

Use the diagram to solve each problem.

Show your work.

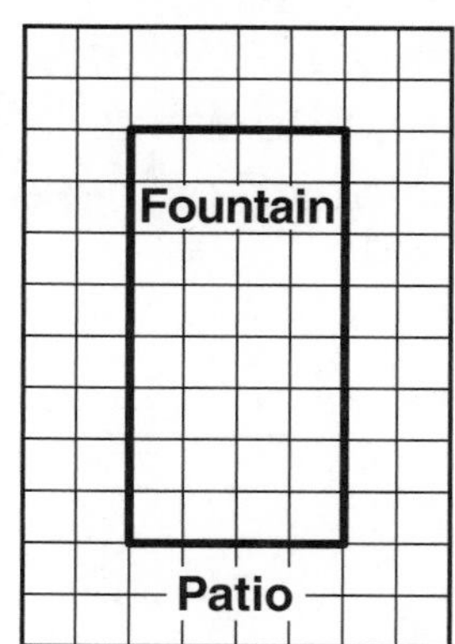

1. The diagram at right shows the design of a tiled patio. The patio surrounds a fountain in Jefferson Park. Each tile on the patio covers 1 square foot. What is the area of the patio, in square feet?

   64 square feet

2. Which has the greater area, the patio or the fountain? How much greater, in square feet?

   The patio; 32 square feet

3. The city is replacing the tiles on the patio around the fountain next year. Each tile costs $4. How much will it cost to replace all the tiles?

   $256

4. **Predict** The new patio will have alternating black and white tiles. How many of each color tile should the city planners buy?

   32 of each color

5. **What If?** Suppose the city adds a border of blue tiles around the outside of the patio. The border will be 1 tile wide. The blue tiles are the same size as the tiles on the patio. How many tiles will be needed to make the border?

   44 tiles

Name ____________________ Date ____________

Problem Solving 17.5

Problem-Solving Application: Use Measurement

Problem Karen has only 12 feet of fencing to mark the perimeter of her garden. She wants her garden to have the greatest area possible. Which of these three garden plans should she use?

1 foot
1 foot

Plan A **Plan B** **Plan C**

1. What do you want to know?

which garden plan Karen should use

PLAN

2. How will you use the perimeters and areas you measure to solve the problem?

I will find the garden with the greatest area that has a perimeter of 12 feet.

SOLVE

3. Which garden plans have perimeters of 12 feet? Which of those garden plans has the greatest area?

Plan A and Plan B; Plan A

4. Plan C has the greatest area. Why didn't you choose it for Karen's garden?

because it does not have a perimeter of 12 feet

Use with text pages 474–475.

Name ______________________ Date ____________

Explore Volume

For Problems 1–4, use the unit cubes shown in each box to estimate the volume of that box. Then use your estimates to solve Problems 5–6.

1. **Fawn's Box**

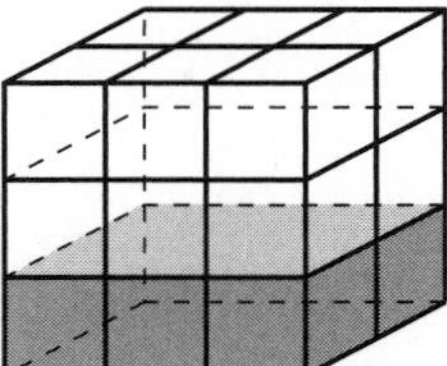

18 unit cubes

2. **Micah's Box**

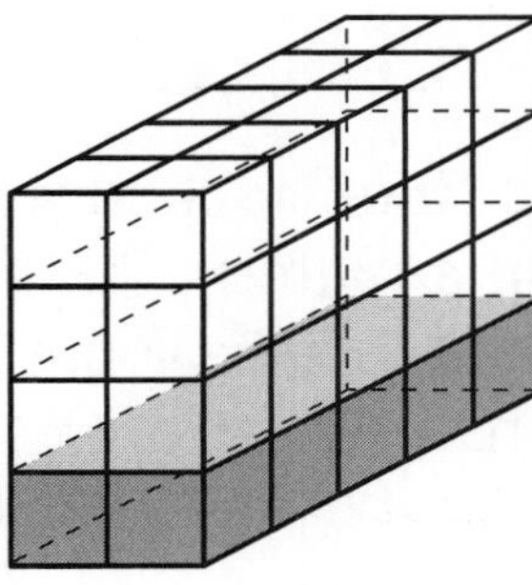

40 unit cubes

3. **Joey's Box**

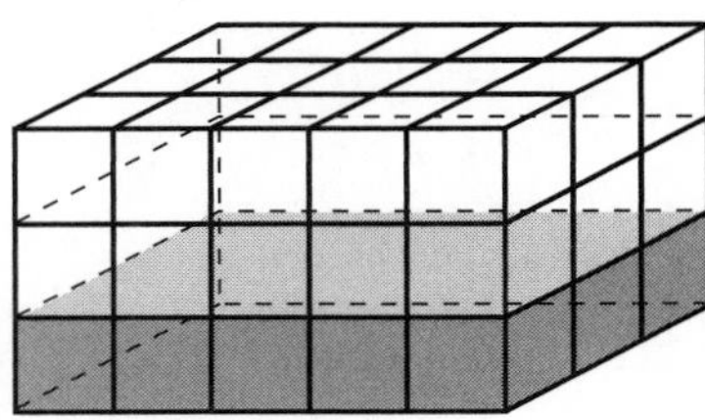

45 unit cubes

4. **Rachel's Box**

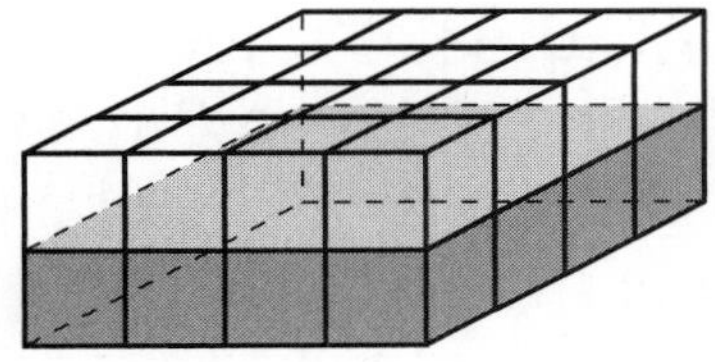

32 unit cubes

5. Whose box has the greatest volume? Whose box has the least volume?

Joey; Fawn

6. **Reasoning** Can two of Fawn's boxes fit inside any of the other boxes? If yes, which ones?

yes; Micah's and Joey's boxes

Show your work.

Name ______________________ Date ____________

Find Volume

Solve each problem. **Show your work.**

1. Jake made this sculpture with wooden blocks. What is the sculpture's volume, in cubic units?

   18 cubic units

2. **Predict** Jake stacked wooden blocks in a pattern. The stack has 5 rows. There are 5 blocks in the bottom row. Each row has 1 fewer block than the row below it. What is the total volume of the blocks that Jake stacked?

   15 cubic units

3. **Reasoning** Jake made an array with his blocks. It had 3 rows with 3 blocks in each row. Then he stacked 2 more of those arrays on top of the first array. What solid figure do the stacked arrays form? What is the volume of the figure?

   a cube; 27 cubic units

4. **What's Wrong?** Jake says that the volume of this sculpture he made with his wooden blocks is 12 cubic units. What mistake did he make? What is the correct volume?

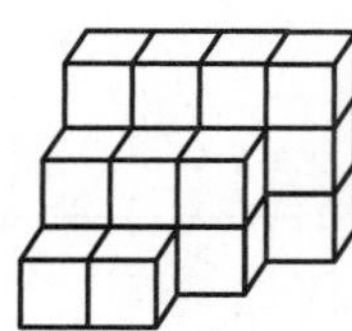

   He did not count the blocks hidden from view by other blocks. The correct volume is 20 cubic units.

Name ______________________ Date ____________

Fractions and Regions

Solve each problem.

1. The national flag of France is shown on the right. What fraction of the flag is red?

   $\frac{1}{3}$

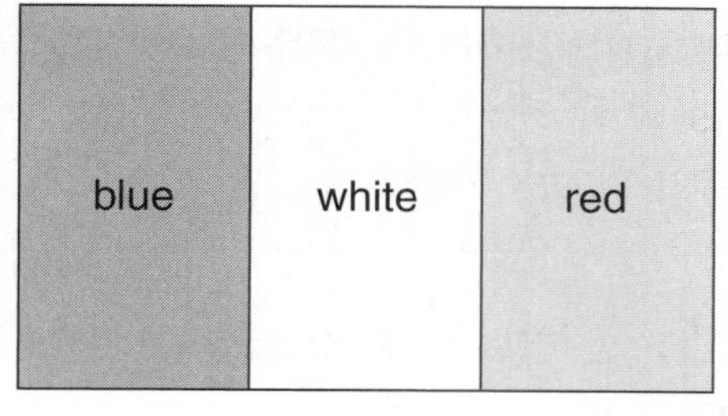

2. **Represent** The French and Italian flags are identical, except that the Italian flag is green where the French flag is blue. What fraction of the Italian flag is white? Draw and color a picture of the national flag of Italy.

   $\frac{1}{3}$; Check students' drawings.

3. The national flag of Nigeria is shown on the right. What fraction of the flag is green?

   $\frac{2}{3}$

green
white
green

4. **Estimate** The national flag of Columbia is shown on the right. About what fraction of the flag is yellow?

   about $\frac{1}{2}$

yellow
blue
red

5. **What's Wrong?** Erica says that $\frac{1}{5}$ of the national flag of Thailand shown on the right is blue. What's wrong?

   The colored regions of the flag are not equal. $\frac{1}{5}$ means one part of 5 equal parts.

red
white
blue
white
red

Use with text pages 498–499.

Name ________________________ Date ______________

Problem Solving 18.2

Fractions and Groups

Use the sheet of stickers at right to solve Problems 1–5.

1. What fraction of the stickers are star stickers?

   $\frac{4}{15}$

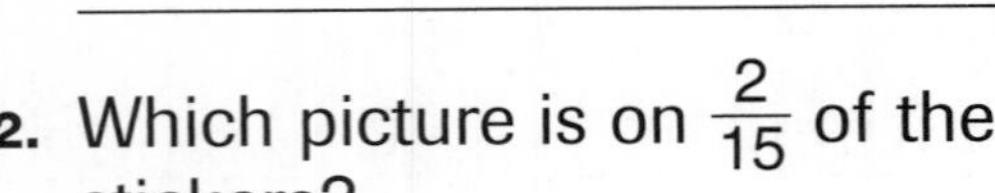

2. Which picture is on $\frac{2}{15}$ of the stickers?

   an arrow

3. What fraction of the stickers are number stickers?

   $\frac{1}{15}$

4. **What If?** Suppose all the star stickers were removed. What fraction of the stickers would be flowers?

   $\frac{1}{11}$

5. **What's Wrong?** Sandy says that $\frac{15}{7}$ of the stickers are heart stickers. What's wrong?

   She reversed the numerator and the denominator. She should say $\frac{7}{15}$ of the stickers are hearts.

Name ______________________ Date ____________

Problem Solving 18.3

Fractional Parts of a Group

Use Data The pictograph below shows how many of each color bead came in Tommy's bead kit. Use the pictograph to solve each problem.

1. Tommy did not use $\frac{3}{4}$ of the green beads in his kit. How many green beads did he use?

   2 green beads

2. If Tommy uses $\frac{2}{3}$ of all the red beads in his kit to make a necklace, how many red beads will he use?

   8 red beads

3. Half of the yellow beads are round, and $\frac{1}{4}$ are oval. The rest of the yellow beads are square. How many yellow beads are square?

   4 yellow beads

4. **Reasoning** Tommy used $\frac{1}{4}$ of all the beads of one color to make earrings. He used 5 beads in all. Which color bead did he use?

   black

5. Tommy used $\frac{2}{5}$ of the blue beads and $\frac{3}{8}$ of the green beads to make a key chain. How many of each color bead did he use? How many beads did he use in all to make the key chain?

   4 blue beads and 3 green beads; 7 beads in all

Bead Kit

Color	Beads
Red	6 bead symbols
Blue	5 bead symbols
Yellow	8 bead symbols
Green	4 bead symbols
Black	10 bead symbols
White	3 bead symbols

Each bead symbol stands for 2 beads.

Show your work.

Name ______________________ Date ______________

Problem Solving 18.4

Problem-Solving Application: Multistep Problems

Problem Sharon bought 8 yards each of calico, polka dot, and denim material. She used $\frac{3}{4}$ of all the cloth to make pillows. How many yards of cloth did she use in all?

1. What do you know?

the amount of cloth Sharon used in all

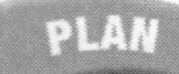

2. What should you do first to solve the problem?

Find the total amount of cloth Sharon bought.

3. How many yards of cloth did Sharon buy in all?

3 fabrics, 8 yards each or $8 \times 3 = 24$ yards

4. What is $\frac{1}{4}$ of the total yards of cloth Sharon bought?

$\frac{1}{4}$ of $24 = 6$ yards

5. How many yards of cloth did Sharon use in all?

$24 - 6 = 18$ yards

6. How can using counters help you check that your answer is reasonable?

Check students' explanations.

Name ______________________ Date ____________

Problem Solving 18.5

Model Equivalent Fractions

Solve each problem.

Show your work.

1. **Represent** What fraction of the sections on Spinner A are shaded? How many sections does Spinner B have? Shade sections of Spinner B so that both spinners have an equivalent fraction of shaded sections.

$\frac{3}{6}$ or $\frac{1}{2}$; 12 sections

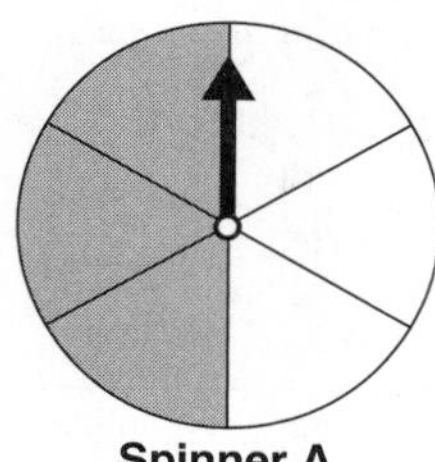

Spinner A

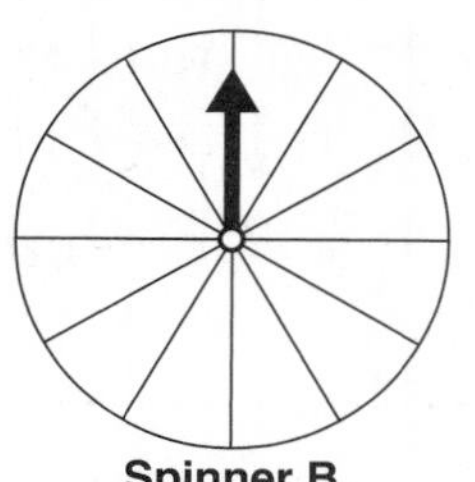

Spinner B

Check students' drawings.

2. **Represent** What fraction of the sections on Bookmark #2 are shaded? How many sections does the Bookmark #1 have? Shade sections of Bookmark #1 so that both bookmarks have an equivalent fraction of shaded sections.

$\frac{1}{5}$; 10 sections

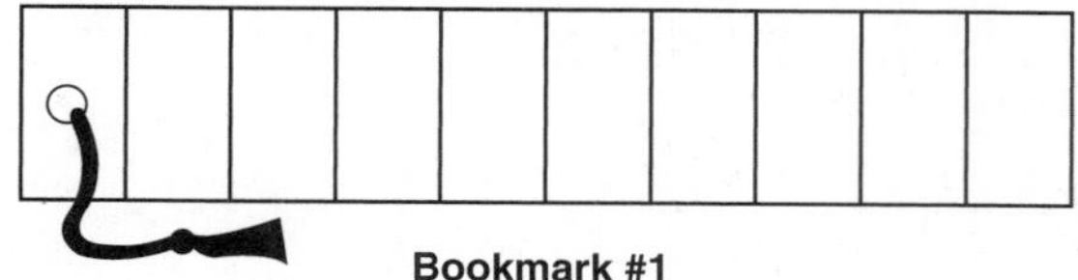

Bookmark #1

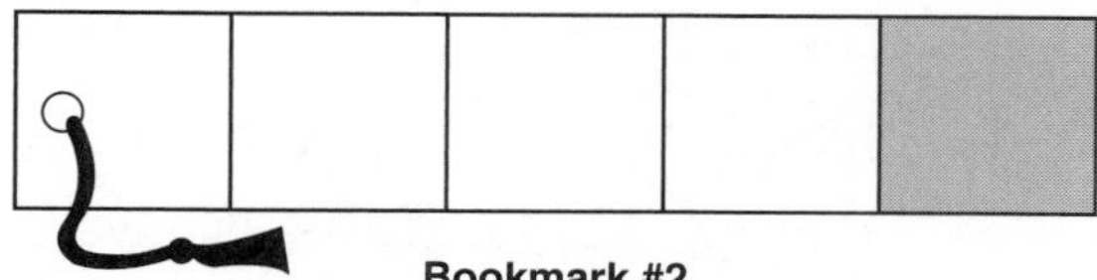

Bookmark #2

Check students' drawings.

3. **What's Wrong?** Bill made the two potholders shown on the right. He says that they show equivalent fractions, because they have an equal number of black squares. What's wrong?

They do not have an equal total number of squares.

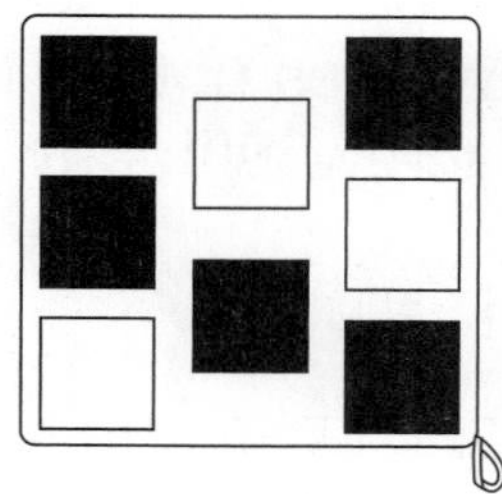

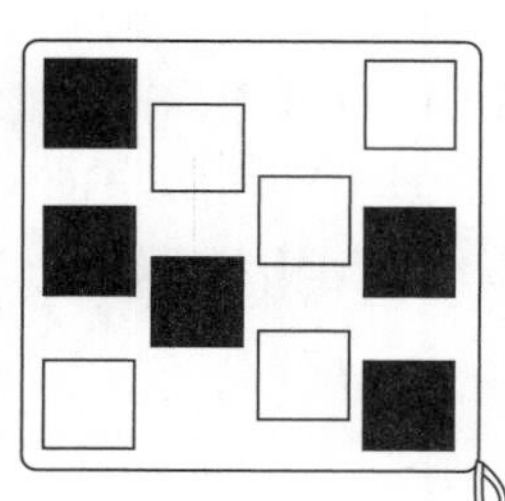

4. **Reasoning** Sally has $\frac{1}{2}$ of a dollar in dimes. Ben has an equivalent fraction of a dollar in quarters. How many quarters does he have?

2 quarters

Use with text pages 508–509.

Name ______________________ Date ____________

Find Equivalent Fractions

Use the table below to solve each problem.

Screw Lengths	
Phillips Head Screw	**Flat Head Screw**
$\frac{1}{8}$ inch	$\frac{3}{12}$ inch
$\frac{1}{2}$ inch	$\frac{7}{8}$ inch
$\frac{1}{4}$ inch	$\frac{4}{8}$ inch
$\frac{3}{5}$ inch	$\frac{2}{16}$ inch
$\frac{3}{8}$ inch	$\frac{6}{10}$ inch

1. Which flat head screw is the same length as the Phillips head screw that is $\frac{1}{8}$ inch long?

   $\frac{2}{16}$ inch flat head screw

2. Which Phillips head screw is the same length as the flat head screw that is $\frac{6}{10}$ inch long?

   $\frac{3}{5}$ inch Phillips head screw

3. Which Phillips head screw does not have a flat head screw with an equivalent length?

   $\frac{3}{8}$ inch Phillips head screw

4. Which flat head screw does not have a Phillips head screw with an equivalent length?

   $\frac{7}{8}$ inch flat head screw

5. **Reasoning** I am a flat head screw. My length is equivalent to the Phillips head screw that is $\frac{1}{2}$ inch long. My numerator and denominator are both even numbers. Which screw am I?

   $\frac{4}{8}$ inch flat head screw

Name ____________________ Date ____________

Problem Solving 18.7

Mixed Numbers

Use the recipes below to solve each problem.

Play Dough Recipe

Mix:

$2\frac{1}{2}$ cups flour

$1\frac{1}{4}$ cups salt

$1\frac{1}{3}$ cups boiling water

$2\frac{2}{3}$ tablespoons oil

Modeling Clay Recipe

Mix:

$3\frac{3}{4}$ cups potato or corn starch

$1\frac{7}{8}$ cups salt

$1\frac{2}{3}$ cups boiling water

Show your work.

1. Which recipe uses $\frac{5}{4}$ cups of salt?

play dough

2. Which recipe uses $\frac{5}{3}$ cups of boiling water?

modeling clay

3. **Reasoning** How can you use a $\frac{1}{4}$ cup measuring cup to measure the amount of potato or corn starch needed for the modeling clay recipe?

Fill the $\frac{1}{4}$ cup 15 times.

4. **Reasoning** How many times will you have to fill a $\frac{1}{3}$ tablespoon measuring spoon to measure the amount of oil needed for the play dough recipe?

8 times

5. **Write About It** Could you use a $\frac{1}{4}$ cup measuring cup to measure the amount of salt needed for the modeling clay recipe? Explain.

Answers may vary.

Name ________________________ Date ____________

Problem Solving 19.1

Compare Fractions

Use the pictures below to solve each problem.

1. What fraction of Brian's pizza has pepperoni? What fraction of Nathan's pizza has pepperoni? Whose pizza has a greater fraction of pepperoni?

   $\frac{2}{6}$; $\frac{8}{10}$; Nathan's

2. What fraction of Carol's pizza has pepperoni? What fraction of Maria's pizza has pepperoni? Whose pizza has a greater fraction of pepperoni?

   $\frac{8}{10}$; $\frac{4}{8}$; Carol's

3. Who has the smallest fraction of plain pizza, Greg, Brian, or Carol?

   Carol

4. All the pizzas are the same size. Whose pizza has the bigger slices, Janet's or Brian's?

   Brian's

5. **What's Wrong?** Maria says that her pizza has a greater fraction of pepperoni than Greg's has, because her pizza has more slices of pepperoni. What's wrong?

   Answers may vary.

Janet's Pizza | Brian's Pizza | Maria's Pizza | Nathan's Pizza | Carol's Pizza | Greg's Pizza

Show your work.

Use with text pages 520–521.

Name ________________________ Date ____________

Problem Solving 19.2

Order Fractions

Curry powder is a blend of spices used in many Indian and African dishes. Use Veda's recipe for curry powder shown below to solve each problem.

Curry Powder Recipe
$2\frac{1}{2}$ tablespoons fenugreek
$\frac{3}{4}$ tablespoon cumin seeds
$\frac{4}{5}$ tablespoon mustard seeds
$\frac{1}{2}$ tablespoon cloves
$3\frac{1}{2}$ tablespoons coriander seeds
$\frac{3}{8}$ tablespoon cinnamon
$1\frac{1}{2}$ tablespoons cardamom seeds
$\frac{1}{4}$ tablespoon mace
$\frac{1}{2}$ tablespoon nutmeg
$\frac{1}{8}$ tablespoon cayenne pepper
1 tablespoon turmeric
$\frac{5}{8}$ tablespoon black pepper

Show your work.

1. Order the amounts of cinnamon, black pepper, and cayenne pepper used in the recipe from least to greatest. cayenne, cinnamon, black pepper

2. Which spice makes up a larger part of the curry powder, mace, nutmeg, or cayenne pepper?

   nutmeg

3. Order the amounts of cloves, mace, and cumin seeds used in the recipe from least to greatest. mace, cloves, cumin seeds

4. **You Decide** Veda says that she does not have to compare fractions to order the amounts of coriander seeds, cardamom seeds, and fenugreek used in the recipe. Do you agree? Explain why or why not.

   Yes; *Explanations may vary.*

5. **Represent** Veda used the fraction strips on the right to order the amounts of three ingredients in the recipe. What ingredients are they?

   cinnamon, cumin seeds, mustard seeds

$\frac{1}{8}$	$\frac{1}{8}$	$\frac{1}{8}$					

$\frac{1}{4}$	$\frac{1}{4}$	$\frac{1}{4}$	

$\frac{1}{5}$	$\frac{1}{5}$	$\frac{1}{5}$	$\frac{1}{5}$	

Name ______________________ Date ____________

Problem Solving 19.3

Problem-Solving Strategy: Act It Out

Problem **Mei, Willis, and Adi made 20 fortune cookies for Multicultural Day. Mei wrote $\frac{2}{5}$ of the fortunes for the cookies. Willis wrote $\frac{1}{2}$ of the fortunes, and Adi wrote $\frac{1}{10}$ of the fortunes. Who wrote the most fortunes for the cookies? Use fraction strips if you wish.**

UNDERSTAND

1. What do you want to know?

   who wrote the most fortunes

PLAN

2. What will you do with your fraction strip models to solve the problem?

   Order the lengths of the fraction strip models.

SOLVE

3. Who wrote the most of the fortunes for the cookies?

   Willis wrote the most fortunes.

LOOK BACK

4. Use 20 counters as models to act out the problem and find how many fortunes they each wrote. How do your results help you check your solution? Mei wrote 8 fortunes; Willis wrote 10 fortunes; Adi wrote 2 fortunes. $10 > 8 > 2$.

Name ____________________ Date ____________

Problem Solving 19.4

Add Fractions

For Multicultural Day, students made soups to celebrate their family heritages. Solve each problem about the soups they made.

Show your work.

1. Olga made borscht, a beet soup popular in Russia. Her soup had $\frac{5}{8}$ pound of shredded beets and $\frac{2}{8}$ pound of shredded cabbage. How much beets and cabbage did Olga use in all?

   $\frac{7}{8}$ pound

2. Diego's grandparents are from Mexico. He made chicken tortilla soup with $\frac{3}{5}$ cup of chopped chicken and $\frac{1}{5}$ cup of chopped tortillas. How many cups of chicken and tortillas did he use in all?

   $\frac{4}{5}$ cup

3. Shana made Irish stew with $\frac{3}{4}$ pound of cubed beef and $\frac{1}{4}$ pound of cubed potatoes. How many pounds of beef and potatoes did she use in the stew?

   $\frac{4}{4}$ pound, or 1 pound

4. **Reasoning** Angela's father is from Italy. She used his recipe to make minestrone soup. The recipe called for $\frac{3}{4}$ cup sliced tomatoes, $\frac{1}{4}$ cup sliced carrots, and $\frac{1}{2}$ cup sliced zucchini. Did she use more or less than 1 cup of sliced vegetables? Explain.

   She used more than 1 cup, because $\frac{3}{4} + \frac{1}{4} =$ 1 and $1 + \frac{1}{2} = 1\frac{1}{2}$ cups in all.

Use with text pages 528–530.

Name ______________________ Date ____________

Problem Solving 19.5

Subtract Fractions

The third-graders used the recipes below to make Native American desserts for Multicultural Day. Use the recipes to solve each problem.

Cherokee Blackberry Cobbler	
$\frac{1}{4}$ quart blackberries	$\frac{3}{6}$ cup honey
1 cup corn meal	$\frac{2}{16}$ cup butter
$\frac{1}{3}$ cup milk	1 egg, slightly beaten

Crow Chokeberry Pudding	
$\frac{2}{4}$ quart chokecherries	$\frac{1}{6}$ cup honey
$\frac{1}{4}$ cup corn meal	4 cups water
$\frac{2}{6}$ cup milk	$\frac{1}{4}$ cup flour

1. Which recipe uses more berries? How much more?

   Crow chokeberry pudding; $\frac{1}{4}$ quart

2. Which recipe uses more honey? How much more?

   Cherokee blackberry cobbler; $\frac{2}{6}$ cup

3. **You Decide** Gilbert says that the pudding recipe uses $\frac{1}{3}$ cup more milk than the cobbler recipe. Do you agree? Explain why or why not.

   No. *Explanations will vary.*

4. **You Decide** To find how much more corn meal is used in the cobbler, Nancy subtracted $\frac{4}{4} - \frac{1}{4} = \frac{3}{4}$. Did she get the correct result? Explain.

   Yes. *Explanations will vary.*

5. The blackberry cobbler recipe makes 8 equal servings. Nina, Jack, and Cameron each ate $\frac{1}{4}$ of the servings. How many servings of cobbler were left over?

   2 servings

Show your work.

Name ______________________ Date ____________

Problem Solving 20.1

Tenths

Use Data Six students each painted a section of the playground fence for a Fourth of July celebration. Each section had 10 fence posts. The table below shows how they chose to paint their fence sections. Use the table to solve each problem.

Playground Fence Painting			
Painter	**Red Posts**	**White Posts**	**Blue Posts**
Annie	7	2	1
Chun	1	3	6
Felipe	9	0	1
Hans	1	8	1
Matt	4	3	3
Nicole	3	5	2

Show your work.

1. What fraction of her fence posts did Annie paint red? What is that fraction written as a decimal?

   $\frac{7}{10}$; 0.7

2. Who painted equal parts of his or her fence posts red and blue? What fraction and decimal names that part?

   Hans; $\frac{1}{10}$; 0.1

3. **Reasoning** Who painted more than five tenths of his or her fence posts blue?

   Chun

4. Which two students painted the same fraction of their fence posts white? What decimal describes each of their white parts?

   Chun and Matt; 0.3

5. **Reasoning** How do you write the part of Felipe's fence section that is painted white as a decimal?

   0.0

Name ______________________ Date ____________

Hundredths

Use Data Amanda surveyed 100 students to find out their favorite item on the playground. She displayed her results on the bar graph shown below. Use the graph to solve each problem.

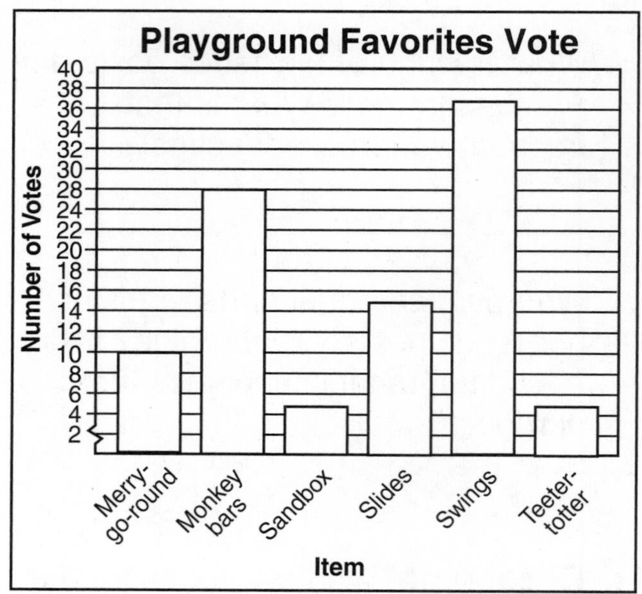

1. Which playground item got the most votes? What decimal represents that part of the total votes?

   swings; 0.37

2. Which item got fifteen hundredths of the votes?

   slides

3. **Reasoning** Which two items got 0.25 of the total votes altogether?

   merry-go-round and slides

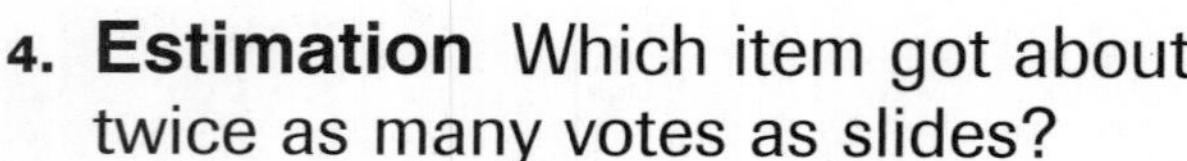

4. **Estimation** Which item got about twice as many votes as slides?

   monkey bars

5. **You Decide** Kay says that the merry-go-round got 0.10 of the votes. Mohammed says that it got 0.1 of the votes. Who is right? Explain.

   Possible answer: They are both right because 0.10 = 0.1.

Name ______________________ Date ____________

Decimals Greater Than 1

The map below shows the length of each nature trail at Forest Park and Playground. Use the map to solve each problem.

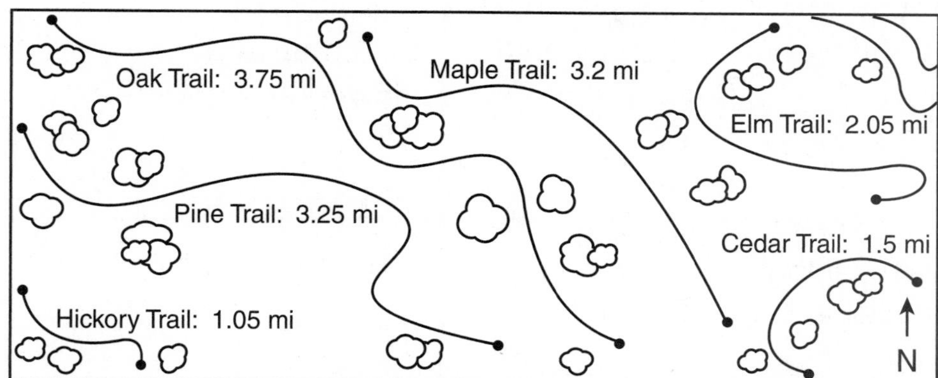

1. Which trail is three and seventy-five hundredths miles long? How do you write that length as a mixed number?

   Oak Trail; $3\frac{75}{100}$ miles

2. **What's Wrong?** Neil says that the Cedar Trail is one and five hundredths mile long. What mistake did Neil make?

   It is one and five tenths miles long.

3. **Reasoning** This trail's length has zero tenths. It is more than 2 miles long. Which trail is it?

   Elm Trail

4. **Reasoning** Which trail is five hundredths of a mile longer than Maple Trail?

   Pine Trail

5. Which trail is $1\frac{5}{100}$ miles long? How do you write that length in words?

   Hickory Trail; one and five hundredths miles

6. **You Decide** Mick says that the Maple Trail is $3\frac{2}{10}$ miles long. Fatima says that it is $3\frac{20}{100}$ miles long. Who is right? Explain your choice.

   They are both right because $3.2 = 3\frac{2}{10} = 3\frac{20}{100}$.

Name ______________________ Date ____________

Problem Solving 20.4

Problem-Solving Decision: Reasonable Answers

Problem Eliot and Christina volunteered to plant a crate of flowers around their neighborhood playground. By noon, they had each planted $\frac{3}{8}$ of the flowers from the crate. They decide that they have half of the crate of the flowers left to plant. Is this reasonable?

UNDERSTAND

1. What information given in the problem will you use to decide if the decision is reasonable? They each planted $\frac{3}{8}$ of the flowers. They say they have $\frac{1}{2}$ of the flowers left to plant.

PLAN

2. Once you find how many flowers they have left to plant, what do you need to do to decide if their decision is reasonable?
Compare that amount to $\frac{1}{2}$.

SOLVE

3. Is the fraction of flowers they planted altogether equivalent to $\frac{1}{2}$? Is their decision reasonable? Explain.
No; no; They planted more than $\frac{1}{2}$ of the flowers. So, they have less than $\frac{1}{2}$ of the flowers left to plant.

LOOK BACK

4. How can thinking that the crate held 8 flowers help you decide if their decision is reasonable? $\frac{3}{8}$ of 8 is 3. They planted 6 flowers in all, so they have 2 flowers left to plant. Half of 8 is 4, and $2 < 4$.

Name ______________________ Date ____________

Problem Solving 20.5

Compare and Order Decimals

Solve each problem about the Jamboree Playground.

Show your work.

1. The Jamboree Playground is 0.31 mile long and 0.13 mile wide. Which is greater, the playground's length or width?

   its length

2. The playground has a blue slide and red slide. The blue slide is 5.6 feet long. The red slide is 5.8 feet long. Which slide is longer?

   the red slide

3. The swing seats at the playground are three different sizes. Their widths are 0.86 meter, 0.60 meter, and 0.68 meter. Order the seat widths from least to greatest.

   0.60 meter, 0.68 meter, 0.86 meter

4. There are four sliding poles in the playground. They are 2.02 meters, 2.00 meters, and 2.20 meters tall. Order the heights of the poles from greatest to least.

   2.20 meters, 2.02 meters, 2.00 meters

5. The playground sandbox has a volume of 5.6 cubic meters. Will two 3-cubic meter bags of sand be enough to fill the sandbox? Explain.

   Yes, because $3 + 3 = 6$ and $6 > 5.6$.

Name ______________________ Date ____________

Problem Solving 20.6

Compare and Order Fractions and Decimals

Use Data Megan and Stu are training for a race. They recorded the distances they walked each day in the tables shown below. Use the tables to solve each problem.

Megan's Walking Log	
Day	**Distance**
Monday	$2\frac{3}{10}$ mi
Tuesday	0.5 mi
Wednesday	1.75 mi
Thursday	$2\frac{1}{4}$ mi
Friday	0.95 mi
Saturday	$1\frac{3}{4}$ mi
Sunday	2.4 mi

Stu's Walking Log	
Day	**Distance**
Monday	0.6 mi
Tuesday	$\frac{1}{2}$ mi
Wednesday	$1\frac{1}{2}$ mi
Thursday	2.2 mi
Friday	$\frac{9}{10}$ mi
Saturday	1.08 mi
Sunday	$2\frac{1}{2}$ mi

Show your work.

1. Who walked the farthest on Friday?

   Megan

2. Who walked the farthest on Sunday?

   Stu

3. On which day did Megan and Stu walk the same distance?

   Tuesday

4. Megan walked the same distance on which 2 days?

   Wednesday and Saturday

5. **Represent** What is the longest distance Megan and Stu each walked? Draw and shade models to compare those distances. Which is greater?

   Megan: 2.4 mi; Stu: $2\frac{1}{2}$ mi; $2\frac{1}{2} > 2.4$; *Check students' models.*

Use with text pages 550–551.

Name ______________________ Date __________

Relate Decimals, Fractions, and Money

Solve each problem.

Check students' work.

1. What is the total value of the coins shown on the right? Write that amount as a fraction of a dollar and as a decimal with a dollar sign.

   52¢; $\frac{52}{100}$; $0.52

2. **Predict** What coin is used to make this table of values? Use the patterns in the table to complete it.

   a nickel

1 coin	2 coins	3 coins	4 coins	5 coins
$0.05	$0.10	$0.15	$0.20	$0.25
$\frac{1}{20}$	$\frac{1}{10}$	$\frac{15}{100}$	$\frac{1}{5}$	$\frac{1}{4}$

3. **Reasoning** Christina found two coins in the playground. One coin had a value of $\frac{1}{10}$ of a dollar. The other had a value of $\frac{1}{4}$ of a dollar. What two coins did she find?

   a dime and a quarter

4. Alex has 1 half-dollar, 1 quarter, 1 dime, 1 nickel, and 1 penny. He wants to buy an ice cream cone that costs $\frac{9}{10}$ of a dollar. Does he have enough money? Explain.

   Yes, because the total value of his coins is $\frac{91}{100}$ and $\frac{91}{100} > \frac{9}{10}$.

5. **Represent** Which amount of money can you show on the model at right, $0.36, $0.30, or $0.63? Explain your choice. Then shade the model to show the amount you chose.

   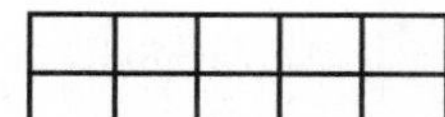

   $0.30, because the other two amounts need a hundredths grid to model.

Name ______________________ Date __________

Add and Subtract Decimals

Use the sales advertisement below to solve each problem.

Show your work.

1. Which slide is taller, the tube or the wave? How much longer?

   The tube, 0.22 m

2. Which slide is longer, the glider or the cyclone? How much longer?

   The cyclone; 2.6 m

3. How much will it cost in all to buy the a glider and a wave slide?

   $206.74

4. How much more does the cyclone slide cost than the tube slide?

   $30.45

5. **What's Wrong?** What is wrong with Emily's work shown on the right?

   She did not regroup the tenths. The correct difference is 0.22 m.

Emily

$$\begin{array}{r} 2.3 \\ -2.08 \\ \hline 0.38 \end{array}$$

The tube is 0.38 meters taller than the wave slide.

Name ______________________ Date ____________

Problem Solving 20.9

Problem-Solving Application: Use Money

Problem The neighborhood planning committee had a bake sale to raise money for new equipment for their playground. The price list for the bake sale is shown at the right. Adrian bought a granola bar and a lemon tart at the bake sale. He paid with a ten-dollar bill. How much change did he receive?

PLAYGROUND BAKE SALE

Cookies: $0.39 each
Granola Bars: $1.99 each
Cupcakes: $1.50 each
Tarts: $3.50 each
Muffins: $2.75 each

1. What information to do need to gather from the price list?

The prices of the granola bar and lemon tart

PLAN

2. What operation will you use to find the amount Adrian spent? What operation will you use to find how much change he should receive?

addition; subtraction

SOLVE

3. How much change did Adrian receive?

$4.51

LOOK BACK

4. How can you count up to check that your change is correct?

Start at the total cost of the purchase and count up by coins and bills to $10.00.

Name ____________________ Date ____________

Problem Solving 21.1

Multiply Multiples of 10, 100, and 1,000

Solve each problem.

Show your work.

1. Toy City just received a shipment of 9 boxes of yo-yos. Each box holds 600 yo-yos. How many yo-yos are in the shipment altogether? What basic fact did you use to find your product?

   5,400 yo-yos; 9 × 6 = 54

2. Each yo-yo costs $3. Toy City sold 40 yo-yos in June and 400 yo-yos in July. What was the total value of those yo-yo sales? What basic fact did you use to find your answer?

   $1,320; 4 × 3 = 12

3. Toy City ordered 6 boxes of slinkies. Each box has 700 slinkies. The store needs 5,000 slinkies in stock for a big sale. How many more slinkies should be ordered? How do you know?

   800 more slinkies, 700 × 6 = 4,200 and 5,000 − 4,200 = 800

4. **What's Wrong?** Toy City has 8 boxes of pogo sticks in its warehouse. Each box has 50 pogo sticks. The store manager says that there are 4,000 pogo sticks in the warehouse. What's wrong?

   Possible answer: 8 × 50 = 400, not 4,000.

5. **Predict** In 10 jumps on his pogo stick, Jamie covered a distance of 20 feet. In 100 jumps, he went 200 feet. In 1,000 jumps, he went 2,000 feet. Predict the distance that Jamie covers with each jump on his pogo stick.

   2 feet

Use with text pages 580–581.

Name ________________________ Date ____________

Problem Solving 21.2

Model Multiplication

Solve each problem. Use base-ten blocks to help you.

Show your work.

1. Kevin reads 16 pages of a book every hour. How many pages will he read in three hours?

   48 pages

2. Eileen reads 3 books each month. How many books will she read in one year?

   36 books

3. Carmen can type 15 pages a day. How many pages can she type in a 5-day work week?

   75 pages

4. **Write About It** To find 4 × 29, Clarence multiplied 4 × 20. Then he multiplied 4 × 9. Then he added his two products. Do you think his method worked? Explain.

   Yes, *Explanations will vary.*

Name ______________________ Date ____________

Problem Solving 21.3

Estimate Products

The table below shows the amounts of some foods the average American eats each year. Use the table to solve each problem.

Average American Yearly Diet	
Food	**Amount**
Bread	46 pounds
Chocolate	13 pounds
Dairy Products	582 pounds
Fish	51 pounds
Fruit	261 pounds
Meat	270 pounds
Potatoes	141 pounds
Sugar	67 pounds
Vegetables	267 pounds

Show your work.

1. On average, about how much chocolate do Americans each eat in 5 years?

   about 50 pounds

2. About how much fish does an average American eat in 3 years?

   about 150 pounds

3. Which food makes up the largest part of most Americans' diets? About how much of that food does the average American eat in 4 years?

   Dairy products;
   about 2,400 pounds

4. In 2 years, about how much more fruit than sugar does the average American eat?

   about 460 pounds more

5. **Multistep** Mr. and Mrs. Johnson have three daughters and two sons. If all the Johnsons eat as many potatoes as the average American, about how much potatoes will the entire family eat this year?

   about 700 pounds

Use with text pages 584–586.

Name ______________________ Date ____________

Problem Solving 21.4

Multiply 2-Digit Numbers by 1-Digit Numbers

Paper was invented in China in A.D. 105 At that time, paper was made from cloth rags. Today, most paper is made from trees. The table below shows how many trees are used to make different kinds of paper.

Use Data Use the table to solve Problems 1–4.

Paper and Trees	
Paper Type	**Number of Trees Used to Make 1 Ton of Paper**
Basic office or Notebook Paper	24
Newspaper	12
Glossy Magazine Paper	15
Catalog Paper (No Gloss)	8

Show your work.

1. How many trees are used to produce 3 tons of basic office paper?

   72 trees

2. A magazine uses 6 tons of glossy paper to print each issue. How many trees are used for each issue?

   90 trees

3. To print its spring catalog, a clothing company uses 91 tons of paper. How many trees are used for the catalog?

   728 trees

4. A local newspaper uses 8 tons of paper to print its Sunday edition. How many trees are needed to produce the Sunday edition?

   96 trees

5. The average person in the United States uses about 62 tons of paper each month. How much does the average person use in 4 months?

   248 tons of paper

Use with text pages 588–590.

Name ______________________ Date ____________

Problem Solving 21.5

Multiply 3-Digit Numbers by 1-Digit Numbers

Solve each problem.

Show your work.

1. The school store sold 4 boxes of pencils last week. Each box had 118 pencils. How many pencils did the store sell last week?

   472 pencils

2. An art supply store sold 243 boxes of pencils last year. Each box cost $3. How much did the store make in all for the pencils sold?

   $729

3. A single pencil can draw a line equal to the length of 616 football fields! How many football fields long would the line be that you used 5 pencils?

   3,080 football fields

4. In a package of pencils, 8 are yellow and 4 are blue. How many yellow pencils are in 426 packages?

   3,408 pencils

5. Enough pencils are produced on Earth each year to circle the moon about 225 times! How many times could the pencils produced in 3 years circle the moon?

   675 times

Use with text pages 592–593.

Name ______________________ Date ______________

Problem Solving 21.6

Problem-Solving Strategy: Solve a Simpler Problem

Problem The first automated photocopier was invented in 1959. This machine took 9 seconds to copy 1 page. Ken needs to make 345 copies of a memo and 258 copies of a flyer. How long would it take him to copy all those pages on the 1959 machine?

UNDERSTAND

1. What do you want to know?

how long it would take Ken to make all his copies

PLAN

2. After you make a simpler problem, what do you need to do to solve the original problem?

Repeat the same steps with the original numbers given in the problem.

SOLVE

3. How long would it take Ken to make all the copies?

5,427 seconds

LOOK BACK

4. Ken used this simpler problem: $3 \times 9 = 27$; $2 \times 9 = 18$; and $27 + 18 = 45$. How can you use it to solve the original problem?

$345 \times 9 = 3{,}105$; $258 \times 9 = 2{,}322$; $3{,}105 + 2{,}322 = 5{,}427$ seconds

Use with text pages 594–596.

Name ______________________ Date ____________

Problem Solving 21.7

Regrouping Twice

The first public library in the United States opened in New England in 1848. It was the first public library that allowed people to borrow books. The table below shows the number of public libraries in New England today.

Use Data Use the table to solve each problem.

New England Public Libraries	
State	**Number of Libraries**
Maine	276
Massachusetts	490
New Hampshire	238
Rhode Island	72
Connecticut	242
Vermont	195

Show your work.

1. If every public library in Rhode Island has 8 atlases, how many atlases do the libraries have in all?

   576 atlases

2. If each public library in Vermont has 2 sets of encyclopedias, how many sets do they have in all?

   390 sets of encyclopedias

3. If every public library in New Hampshire has 4 computers, what is the total number of computers in those libraries?

   952 computers

4. If 6 librarians work in each public library in Connecticut, how many librarians does the state employ?

   1,452 librarians

5. **What's Wrong?** Massachusetts ordered 5 new desks for each of its public libraries. Joan says that 2,050 desks were ordered in all. What's wrong? She did not add her regrouped hundred. 490 × 5 = 2,450: 2,450 desks were ordered in all, not 2,050.

Name ______________________ Date ____________

Problem Solving 21.8

Multiply Money

Use the table to solve each problem.

1. Which item was invented most recently? How much will 7 boxes of that item cost in all?

   Tape; $8.89

2. Donna bought 4 boxes of batteries for her camping trip. How much did she spend in all?

   $16.76

3. Cameron bought 3 boxes of safety pins. He paid with a ten-dollar bill. How much change did he receive?

   $1.03

4. **Reasoning** Shante is buying 8 light bulbs for the track lighting in her kitchen. If each box has 4 light bulbs, how much will she spend in all?

   $7.58

5. **What's Wrong?** Fran did the multiplication at right to find how much 4 boxes of pushpins will cost. What mistake did she make?

   She wrote the decimal incorrectly in her product. The total cost is $12.60.

Small Stuff Store		
Item	**Year Invented**	**Price for 1 box**
Battery	1800	$4.19
Light Bulb	1878	$3.79
Paper Clip	1889	$1.75
Pushpin	1900	$3.15
Safety Pin	1849	$2.99
Tape	1923	$1.27
Zipper	1913	$9.25

Show your work.

Fran

$$\begin{array}{r} \overset{2}{3}15 \\ \times\quad 4 \\ \hline \$1.260 \end{array}$$

4 boxes of pushpins will cost $1.26.

Name ______________________ Date ____________

Problem Solving 22.1

Use Mental Math to Divide

Use the table to solve each problem.

School Fundraisers

Event	Amount Raised
Bake Sale	$270
Car Wash	$560
Carnival	$3,200
Cookie Sale	$540
Flea Market	$4,500
Read-a-Thon	$3,000
Used Book Sale	$360
Walk-a-Thon	$2,100

Show your work.

1. The students charged $7 to wash each car. How many cars did they wash at that fundraiser?

   80 cars

2. Students collected $3 for every mile that they walked in the walk-a-thon. What was the total number of miles that the students walked?

   700 miles

3. Tickets to the school carnival were $8 each. How many people bought tickets to the carnival?

   400 people

4. The read-a-thon lasted 6 months. If the students raised the same amount each month of the read-a-thon, how much did they raise each month?

   $500

5. **Multistep** At the used book sale, each paperback book cost $2. Each hardcover book cost $4. The students sold 40 hardcover books. How many paperback books did they sell?

   100 paperback books

Name ______________________ Date ____________

Problem Solving 22.2

Model Division with Remainders

Solve each problem. Use counters and repeated subtraction to help you.

1. **What's Wrong?** After Mindy used these counters to model a division problem, she said that 37 ÷ 5 = 6 R7. What's wrong?

She can put 1 of the 7 left over counters into each of the 5 groups. 37 ÷ 5 = 7 R2

Show your work.

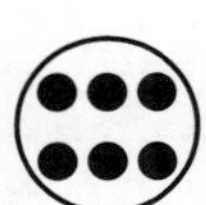
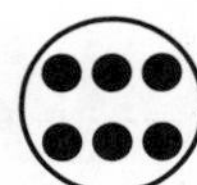
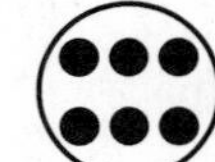

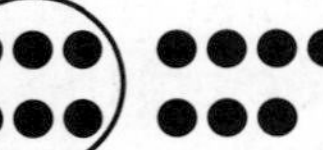

2. **Predict** If you modeled each of the division problems shown below, which would have a remainder? Explain your choice.

24 ÷ 4 24 ÷ 5 24 ÷ 6

24 ÷ 5; *Explanations may vary.*

3. Melissa has 38 dyed eggs. She wants to store them in cartons of 12 eggs each. How many cartons will be full? How many eggs will be in the carton that is not full?

3 cartons; 2 eggs

4. Liam organized 28 video games in boxes. He put 5 games in each box. How many full boxes does he have? How many video games are in the box that is not full?

5 boxes; 3 games

Name ______________________ Date ____________

Problem Solving 22.3

Estimate Quotients

Use the table to solve each problem.

Red Cross Blood Drive

Blood Type	Pints Collected
A negative	115
A positive	638
AB negative	18
AB positive	32
B negative	43
B positive	187
O negative	146
O positive	709

Show your work.

1. There are 2 pints in 1 quart. About how many quarts of A negative blood were collected at the blood drive?

   about 50 quarts

2. Five nurses collected the AB positive blood. Each collected the same amount. About how many pints did they each collect?

   about 6 pints

3. There are 8 pints in 1 gallon. About how many gallons of A positive blood did the blood drive collect?

   about 80 gallons

4. The Red Cross sent the same amount of O negative blood to 3 different hospitals. About how much blood did they send to each hospital?

   about 50 pints

5. **Write About It** The Red Cross sent equal amounts of all the type O blood to 9 blood banks. Jody says they sent about 90 pints to each bank. Carl says they sent about 100 pints to each bank. Why are both estimates reasonable?

   They used different compatible numbers for 855 and 9.

Use with text pages 616–618.

Name ______________________ Date ____________

Problem Solving 22.4

Two-Digit Quotients

Use the table to solve each problem.

Capital City Police Special Units

Unit	Number of Officers
Air Support	39
Bicycle Patrol	85
D.A.R.E.	84
K-9	36
Marine Patrol	30
Mounted Patrol	53
SWAT	69

Show your work.

1. Each of the officers in the air support unit is assigned to one of 3 helicopters. How many officers are assigned to each helicopter?

   13 officers

2. The SWAT unit works in 6 teams. Officers not assigned to a team are on call that week. How many officers are on each SWAT team? How many are on call each week?

   11 officers on each team; 3 officers on call

3. An equal number of D.A.R.E. officers are assigned to each of the 4 school districts in Capital City. How many D.A.R.E. officers serve each district?

   21 officers

4. **Reasoning** The police department plans to double the size of the K-9 unit so that each precinct will have 8 K-9 officers. How many precincts are in the department?

   9 precincts

5. **Write About It** The mounted patrol unit will march in this year's police parade. The police chief wants them to march in equal rows of 5 officers. She figures that there will be 1 row with only 3 officers. Is the chief right? How do you know?

   Yes; Her division is correct: 53 ÷ 5 = 10 R3; So there will be 1 row of 3 officers.

Name ______________________ Date ____________

Problem Solving 22.5

Problem-Solving Application: Interpret Remainders

Problem There are 30 fire inspectors and 8 stations in the Spring Hill Fire Department. Each month, the department assigns an equal number of inspectors to each station. The rest of the inspectors are on call. How many inspectors are assigned to each station?

UNDERSTAND

1. What do you know?

There are 30 inspectors and 8 stations.

PLAN

2. Why should you divide to solve this problem?

To divide the 30 inspectors into 8 equal groups

SOLVE

3. Use words from the problem to describe each part of your division sentence.

Dividend: 30 fire inspectors

Divisor: 8 fire stations

Quotient: 3 inspectors assigned to each station

Remainder: 6 inspectors on call

LOOK BACK

4. Write a question about the fire inspectors for which the remainder is the answer.

Questions will vary.

Use with text pages 622–623.

Name ______________________ Date ____________

Problem Solving 22.6

Three-Digit Quotients

Solve each problem.

Show you work.

1. This month the 342 stream team members will clean up 3 wetland areas. An equal number of members will work in each area. How many stream team members will help clean up each wetland area?

   114 members

2. The Meals-on-Wheels volunteers deliver 791 meals each week. How many meals do they deliver each day?

   113 meals

3. There were 972 huggers volunteering at this year's Special Olympics. The same number of huggers worked at each of the 9 events, and each hugger worked at only one event. How many huggers volunteered at each event?

   108 huggers

4. **What's Wrong?** The third-graders collected 420 blankets this winter to give to homeless shelters. They gave the same number of blankets to 4 different shelters. Janet says that they gave 150 blankets to each shelter. What mistake did she make?

   She wrote the 5 in the wrong place value in her quotient. $420 \div 4 = 105$

Use with text pages 624–625.

Name ________________________ Date ____________

Problem Solving 22.7

Place the First Digit

Use the table to solve each problem.

States with the Fewest Full-Time Firefighters

State	Number of Firefighters
Alaska	586
Delaware	177
Idaho	934
Montana	524
North Dakota	301
South Dakota	389
Vermont	260
West Virginia	896
Wyoming	321

Show your work.

1. If all the firefighters in Wyoming are evenly divided into 3 large departments, how many firefighters are in each department?

   107 firefighters

2. The North Dakota firefighters each volunteer one day a week for community service. If an equal number of firefighters volunteers each day, how many volunteer on Friday?

   43 firefighters

3. The Idaho firefighters give fire safety demonstrations in 9 school districts. About how many firefighters give the demonstrations in each district?

   about 100 firefighters

4. The state of Vermont is divided into 5 regions. If each region has an equal number of firefighters, how many work in each region?

   52 firefighters

5. **Multistep** Each state divides its firefighters into 4 equal groups. One group from each state is sent to help fight a forest fire. How many firefighters from Montana and West Virginia will be sent in all? How did you find your answer?

   355 firefighters; explanations may vary.

Use with text pages 626–627.

Name ______________________ Date ____________

Divide Money

Solve each problem.

Show your work.

1. Bryant raised $9.45 on his first 3 calls for a charity telethon. Each caller pledged the same amount of money. How much did each caller donate to the charity?

   $3.15

2. A pack of 4 cards at the charity bingo game cost $4.60. How much does each bingo card cost?

   $1.15

3. The third-graders sold homemade dog biscuits to raise money for an animal shelter. They charged $2.58 for a box of 6 biscuits. How much did each biscuit cost?

   $0.43

4. Alice sets aside the same amount of money each day to donate to charity. If she donates $8.40 each week to charity, how much money does she set aside each day?

   $1.20

5. **What's Wrong?** Nina and 3 friends want to share a charity raffle ticket that costs $6.28. Look at how Nina found how much they should each pay. What did she do wrong?

   She did not bring down the 2 dimes. $6.28 ÷ 4 = $1.57

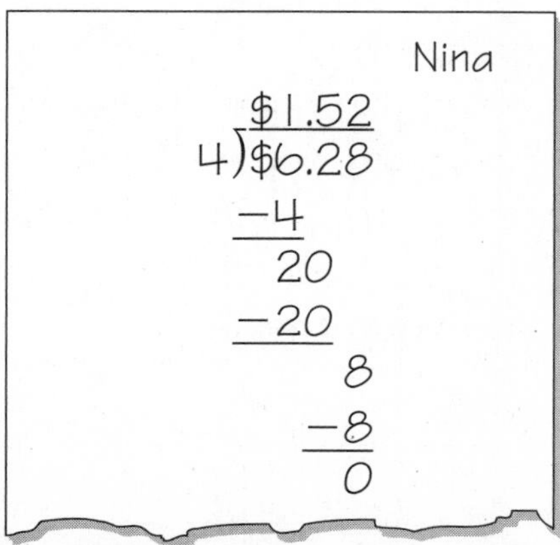

Use with text pages 628–630.